Foreign
Direct
Investment
in China

Winners and Losers

Foreign
Direct
Investment
in China

Winners and Losers

Galina Hale
Federal Reserve Bank of San Francisco, USA

Cheryl Long
Colgate University, USA

 World Scientific

EW JERSEY • LONDON • SINGAPORE • BEIJING • SHANGHAI • HONG KONG • TAIPEI • CHENNAI

Published by

World Scientific Publishing Co. Pte. Ltd.

5 Toh Tuck Link, Singapore 596224

USA office: 27 Warren Street, Suite 401-402, Hackensack, NJ 07601

UK office: 57 Shelton Street, Covent Garden, London WC2H 9HE

British Library Cataloguing-in-Publication Data
A catalogue record for this book is available from the British Library.

FOREIGN DIRECT INVESTMENT IN CHINA
Winners and Losers

ISBN-13 978-981-4340-40-3
ISBN-10 981-4340-40-5

In-house Editor: Dan Jun

Typeset by Stallion Press
Email: enquiries@stallionpress.com

Printed in Singapore and the United States of America.

To our parents

Preface

Over five years of studying the effects of FDI on Chinese markets have led us to organize our findings in this volume. We hope that it will be useful for anyone interested in foreign direct investment (FDI) and the Chinese economy, as well as for those involved in FDI-related policy making. We believe that it is more illuminating to consider the many effects that foreign direct investments have had on the Chinese economy in concert than to focus on them one-by-one. Our work on this volume has provided further support for this view — as we gathered all our findings together and filled in the gaps, we formed a "big picture" view that we are happy to share with the readers.

Many people were instrumental in our studies. First and foremost there are our coauthors. Chapter 3 on FDI spillovers on productivity of domestic firms and parts of chapter 8 came out of the work on a freestanding research paper coauthored with Hiro Miura and encouraged along the way by Ted Moran. Chapter 6 on innovation and imitation is largely based on the paper coauthored with Irene Brambilla and published in the *Scandinavian Journal of Economics*. Much of the work could not have been completed without contributions from Hiro Miura and Chris Candelaria.

Along the way, as we presented our research in bits and pieces, we benefited enormously from comments and encouragement by our colleagues at the NBER China working group led by Shang-Jin Wei, participants at various seminars and conferences, and colleagues at the Federal Reserve Bank of San Francisco and Colgate University.

None of this research would have taken place if not for the generosity of Stanford Center for International Development and Hoover Institution, where the authors were visiting scholars when they first met and started tackling this project in 2005. Financial support of our respective institutions, San Francisco Fed and Colgate University, was also instrumental in facilitating collaboration on this project. Some of the work on this book was conducted while Hale was visiting the Hong Kong Institute of Monetary Research in December 2009, and other parts were completed when Long was visiting the University of Electronic Science and Technology of China in the summers of 2007–2009 as a special term professor. We are grateful for their support.

Anita Todd and Elliot Marks read through many pieces of this work to correct our style and improve the clarity of presentation. Li Xi Dong and Danjun Zheng were extremely competent and patient in facilitating our communication with the publisher and allowing us to focus on the content and sparing us logistical details, for which we are most grateful.

Last, but definitely not least are our friends and families who had to put up with our late working hours, especially in the final stages of the work. Their presence in our lives has provided the foundation on which all of our work is built.

It is important to emphasize that the views that we present in this book are our own and in no way reflect the views of the Federal Reserve Bank of San Francisco, Federal Reserve System, Hong Kong Monetary Authority, or any other institution with which the authors are currently affiliated or were affiliated in the past. All errors are, of course, our own.

Contents

List of Figures

List of Tables

Chapter 1

Introduction and Overview

The worldwide surge in foreign direct investment (FDI) flows during the past decade has stirred up increasing interest in studying the effects of FDI flows on the host countries, including both the performance of foreign-invested firms themselves and the impact of the presence of these foreign-invested firms on indigenous firms. Learning about these effects contributes to the understanding of technological synergies between foreign and domestic firms in the processes of production, innovation, trade, and aggregate economic growth. It also provides valuable information to policy makers in deciding whether FDI should be encouraged with preferential policies and whether foreign firms should be granted special treatment. The most prominent example is that of China, where the surge of economic growth in the last decade has been accompanied by both rapid FDI flows and aggressive government policies aimed at attracting FDI.

How to evaluate the role of FDI in promoting China's economic growth? This book intends to help answer this question by presenting comprehensive findings on how FDI affects both foreign-invested firms and domestic firms in China. In this chapter, we will first give an overview of government policies regarding FDI in China and review the relevant literature, then we will provide an overall description of Chinese manufacturing firms during the 2000–2006 period. Finally, we will give the outline of the current book.[1]

1.1. Foreign Direct Investment and FDI Policies in China

China's FDI policies developed from being prohibitive before 1978 to being permissive in certain area in the early 1980s, then to being encouraging from the mid-1980s to the mid-1990s, and further matured in the mid-1990s to

---

[1]Parts of the text in Sections 1 and 2 of this chapter appeared in Hale and Long (2011).

link FDI to domestic development priorities.[2] With the country's accession
into the World Trade Organization (WTO) in 2001, substantial changes
were further made to its FDI policies largely to unify the treatment of
domestic and foreign firms.

At the beginning of the reform era in the early 1980s, FDI was allowed
only in a limited number of special economic zones (SEZs). Since then the
geographic scope was gradually expanded to cover more coastal cities and
regions, and then finally to include the whole country by the mid-1990s.
Along with the expansion of geographic areas open to FDI, government
policies toward FDI also evolved from merely permissive to encouraging
through favorable treatment in taxes, tariffs, foreign exchange regulations,
and licensing requirements. These early measures, largely embodied in the
*Provisions of the State Council of the People's Republic of China for the
Encouragement of Foreign Investment* (1986), prompted rapid growth in
FDI inflow into China, especially between the mid-1980s and the mid-1990s.

Illustrating the breathtaking speed of FDI growth in China, the annual
FDI inflow was $100 million in 1979, $1 billion in 1984, and then touched
around $40 billion in 1995. As shown in Figure 1.1, the annual FDI inflow

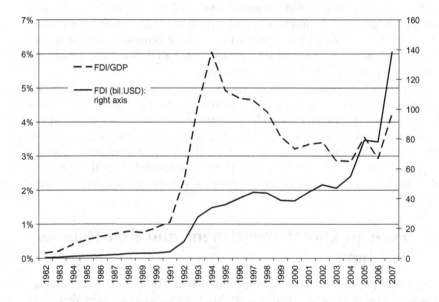

Figure 1.1   FDI inflows into China.
Source: Statistical Yearbook, various issues (Chinese National Bureau of Statistics).

---

[2]Fung, Iizaka, and Tong (2004) provide a detailed review of the trend, policy, and
impact of FDI in China before the 2000s.

has remained above \$40 billion since 1995, while the FDI to GDP ratio has surpassed 3% since 1992. Between 1994 and 1997, the ratio exceeded 5%. Interestingly, Dollar, Hallward-Driemeier, and Mengistae (2006) show that the investment climate in China is superior to that of South Asian or Latin American countries and that this advantage helps explain large FDI inflows into China.

Due to the limited number of geographic regions open to foreign capital and the favorable policies toward export processing firms in the early stages of China's opening up, FDI was largely concentrated in coastal areas and labor-intensive industries. In particular, the southeastern part of China, led by Guangdong and Fujian provinces, received the bulk of foreign capital, which largely came from the Greater China Area such as Hong Kong, Macao, and Taiwan. The targeted industries for investment were largely labor-intensive sectors such as footwear, clothing, and textile.

Since the mid-1990s, in addition to further expanding the geographic regions open to foreign investment and maintaining a favorable investment environment, government policies began to focus more on linking FDI to domestic development priorities. For instance, the *Provisional Guidelines for Foreign Investment Projects*, which took effect in 1995, classified all FDI projects as one of the following four categories: encouraged, restricted, prohibited, and permitted. Priority was given to FDI in the agriculture, energy, transportation, telecommunications, basic raw materials, and high-technology industries. In response, investment from large multinational corporations from outside the Greater China Area has increased rapidly and FDI has started to shift toward capital- and technology-intensive industries since the mid-1990s. Their target regions now cover both the Pearl River delta and the Yangtze River delta, and the industries of choice also have expanded to various capital intensive sectors such as machinery, equipment, electronics, and chemical products.

Beginning 21st this century, China has further adjusted its FDI policies, partly to prepare for its accession into the World Trade Organization (WTO), but also to encourage FDI to help develop the vast West. On one hand, China has opened up more sectors for foreign investment, including retail, wholesale, banking, and telecommunication. On the other hand, projects that could take advantage of the rich natural resources and relatively low labor costs in the central and northwest regions are vigorously encouraged. The new *Guiding Catalogue of Foreign Investment Projects* published in 2002 combined the categories of FDI projects into three: encouraged, prohibited, and permitted.

Although the full effects of these two sets of policies may yet to be realized, the patterns presented later in this chapter will give evidence showing that the impact of the policy changes is already visible. Most importantly,

the underlying message from the above overview of the evolution of FDI
policies in China seems clear: China will continue to attract more FDI inflow
in a more encompassing way as its FDI policies become more transparent
and uniform over time. We expect to see more FDI coming from a greater
diversity of sources into China, covering ever larger geographic areas as well
as an increasingly broader range of economic sectors. FDI will continue to
play an important role in China's growing economy.

1.2. Literature on the Effects of FDI

In spite of China's great success in attracting foreign direct investment, the
effects of FDI on domestic firms are far from clear. For instance, Huang
(2005) argues that the large FDI inflow into China is accompanied by
the repressive policies toward domestic private firms, implying that foreign firms have wrestled resources, markets, and policy preferences away
from domestic firms.

From the viewpoint of the Chinese government, the goal in encouraging FDI has been clearly stated from the very beginning: to obtain
advanced technology as well as management skills from foreign partners.
It was thought, however, that the way to achieve such goals was through
partnering foreign investors with existing Chinese firms. In fact, the government did not allow solely foreign-owned firms until the passage in 1986 of
the *Law of the People's Republic of China on Enterprises Operated Exclu-
sively with Foreign Capital*, suggesting that the Chinese government had
doubts about FDI technology spillover effects on domestic firms. Furthermore, restrictions on domestic sales of foreign-invested firms that existed
during much of the pre-WTO period seem to reflect the government's concern that foreign firms might crowd out domestic firms in their competition
for domestic market share.

In addition to the potential competition effects on the output market,
FDI inflows may also pose competition to domestic firms on the input
markets, especially on the labor market. The latter competition effects may
not have entered the policy makers' minds at the time. But our results
presented below suggest that such competition effects are quite important
and thus deserve more consideration in the future.

From the perspective of academic research, there is a vast body of
academic literature that looks at FDI effects on foreign-invested firms and
domestic firms. These studies usually focus on the measure of total factor productivity (estimated as the residual term in a production function
regression) or labor productivity (computed as the ratio between sales and

employment). They either compare the productivity in foreign firms with that in domestic firms, or explore the relationship between foreign firm presence and the productivity of domestic firms.

Among research work comparing foreign and domestic firms, various studies have shown the productivity advantage in foreign-invested firms. Hasan (2002) and Gupta (2005) provide such evidence for India, Arnold and Javorcik (2009), Bartel and Harrison (2005), and Takii (2004) for Indonesia, Yasar and Paul (2007) for Turkey, Aitken and Harrison (1999) for Venezuela, Akimova and Schwödiauer (2004) for Ukraine, and Karpaty (2007) for Sweden. Published work on China includes Ge and Chen (2008), Lane, Feinberg, and Broadman (2002), Li, Zhou, and Zajac (2009), and Ng and Tuan (2005), and these studies also find that foreign firms are more productive in the case of China. In addition, Ge and Chen (2008) observe variations among foreign firms with capital from different parts of the world. Firms with investment from within the Greater China Area are less likely to experience increased productivity compared to domestic firms than firms with FDI from outside the region.

A larger literature explores the spillover effects of FDI on indigenous firms in the host country. Conceptually, the spillover effects can be broadly categorized into pecuniary effects and "demonstration" effects. Pecuniary channels affect the productive capabilities of domestic firms because the entry of multinational firms leads to more severe competition in the host country market, which is also referred to as competition effect. Such a "competition effect" could be positive, if it provides an incentive for local firms to use their existing resources more efficiently or to search for new technologies, or negative, if local firms suffer a large loss in market share and are not able to keep up technologically, or if their access to inputs and factors of production are restricted. Evidence of a positive competition effect can be found in Blomström and Kokko (1998), while Aitken and Harrison (1999) show the evidence of a negative competition effect of foreign direct investment.

Demonstration effects of FDI refer to situations in which domestic firms can improve their productive efficiency, managerial methods, or product quality, through formal or informal contact with foreign-invested firms. Demonstration externalities may take place through different channels, such as direct observation of production processes, hiring workers previously trained by foreign affiliates, and business transactions with foreign suppliers or clients.

Theoretical work has further explored the more specific mechanisms for FDI spillovers and has generally predicted positive effects of FDI presence on domestic firms' productivity. For example, Kaufmann (1997), Haaker

(1999), Fosfuri, Motta, and Rønde (2001), Glass and Saggi (2002) predict positive same-industry, or horizontal, spillovers through the labor mobility channel, while Wang and Blomström (1992) predict positive spillovers through competition and demonstration effects. In addition, Rodriguez-Clare (1996) outlines forward and backward linkages between foreign firms and domestic firms as a possible mechanism for positive spillovers.

In contrast to the largely unambiguous theoretical predictions, empirical studies on FDI spillovers have produced mixed results. As in studies comparing foreign and domestic firms, the majority of existing empirical studies on externalities from FDI focus on productivity of local firms, usually defined as total factor productivity (TFP). In general, positive spillovers on TFP are found for developed countries. The results are less conclusive in the case of developing economies and seem to favor spillovers taking place through contacts between multinationals and their local suppliers rather than between firms that compete in the same industry.

Specifically, Haskel, Pereira, and Slaughter (2007) consider the case of the UK, Keller and Yeaple (2009) the US, and Peri and Urban (2006) Italy and Germany, and find positive spillovers for these countries. In contrast, Haddad and Harrison (1993), Aitken and Harrison (1999), and Djankov and Hoekman (2000) do not find positive horizontal spillovers in Morocco, Venezuela, and the Czech Republic. More generally, among the 42 studies on intra-industry (horizontal) productivity spillovers of FDI summarized in Görg and Greenaway (2004), only 20 studies report unambiguously positive and significant results, out of which 14 may be subject to biases that lead to overestimates. The results appear more conclusive for vertical spillovers.

On the other hand, positive vertical spillovers are found by Javorcik (2004) for the case of Lithuania, by Schoors and van der Tol (2002) on Hungary, and by Alfaro and Rodríguez-Clare (2004) on Brazil, Chile, Mexico and Venezuela. Similarly, among the five studies discussed in Görg and Greenaway (2004) that focus on vertical FDI spillover effects, three find positive backward FDI spillovers and one finds positive forward FDI spillovers. In particular, Javorcik (2004) and Blalock and Gertler (2008) find positive vertical FDI spillovers in Latvia and Indonesia, a transition economy and a developing country, respectively.

To add to the ambiguity of the findings, studies producing supportive evidence of FDI spillovers may overestimate the effects for three reasons (Hale and Long, 2011). First of all, given that foreign-invested firms are more productive than domestic firms, studies using aggregate data that include foreign firms may exaggerate the positive effects of FDI on domestic firms' productivity (aggregation bias). In addition, studies that include only domestic firms (with firm level data or aggregate data) may face the endogeneity problem: Since FDI is more likely to go to places with higher domestic productivity to begin with, the positive correlation between FDI and productivity of domestic firms may simply reflect the location decision by foreign investors rather than the positive spillover effects of their investment (selection bias). Finally, studies using firm-level data may underestimate the standard errors and thus may mistakenly conclude that the estimates are significant even when they are not, unless robust standard errors are computed (clustered at the level of FDI presence). Since the measure of FDI presence is, by necessity, an aggregate measure, the standard errors in the firm-level regressions are potentially correlated (Moulton, 1990), causing the standard errors to be underestimated (standard error clustering bias).

Accordingly, studies on FDI spillover effects in China have obtained a wide range of estimates and many of them are subject to the three biases discussed above. Depending on the level of data aggregation, studies on FDI spillovers in China can be divided into provincial level studies, industry level studies, and firm level studies. As shown in Hale and Long (2011), two studies at the provincial level (Huang, 2004; Cheung and Lin, 2004) suffer from an upward aggregation bias since they are not able to distinguish domestic firms from foreign-invested firms. The same is true for one of the industry level studies (Liu, Parker, Vaidya, and Wei, 2001). In addition, some of the industry level studies (Liu, 2002) underestimate the standard error on the coefficient of interest, when using the average level of FDI for the manufacturing sector in the city of Shenzhen for all 29 industries in the sample without clustering the standard errors at the city level (Moulton, 1990).

More importantly, all but two studies surveyed in Hale and Long (2011) suffer from potential endogeneity bias, where the correlation obtained between FDI level and productivity may merely reflect the location choice of foreign investors. For example, Chuang and Hsu (2004) use a cross-section of half a million firms, limit their analysis to domestic firms, and aggregate their data to 673 industry–province level cells. Their analysis is not subject to the aggregation bias discussed above, but the positive FDI effects that they find are subject to the endogeneity bias. In fact, studies that analyze the location of FDI in China, including Sun, Tong, and Yu (2002) and Cheng and Kwan (2000), tend to find a positive correlation between per capita gross domestic product (GDP) (positively related to productivity) and FDI. To control for the endogeneity of FDI level, the researcher at the very least needs to either adopt the IV approach by instrumenting FDI level, or to estimate the firm fixed–effects model using panel data of domestic firms. Unfortunately, several studies use the 3SLS model but address the endogeneity of variables other than FDI (Li, Liu, and Parker, 2001; Liu, Parker, Vaidya, and Wei, 2001), while others use the fixed effects model but not with firm fixed effects (Cheung and Lin, 2004; Liu, 2002; Wei and Liu, 2006).

As a result, Hu and Jefferson (2002) and Liu (2008) are the only studies we are aware of that include estimates not subject to the endogeneity problem, and they both find negative or no FDI spillover effects. Hu and Jefferson's study uses 8917 domestic textile firms and 2289 domestic electronic firms and finds negative and significant effects of FDI presence on the TFP of domestic electronic firms. But the more convincing findings are from the authors' panel data analysis of 701 textile firms and 212 electronic firms for 1995–1999, which includes firm fixed effects. If the unobserved factors that determine both the amount of FDI and the productivity of domestic firms are time-invariant, then the estimates of FDI spillovers in Hu and Jefferson (2002) do not suffer from the upward biases outlined above. The results from the FE estimation show negative but insignificant FDI spillover effects. Similarly, Liu (2008) finds negative contemporaneous effects of FDI presence in the same, upstream, and downstream industries on firms' TFP when controlling for firm fixed effects in a five-year panel of almost 20,000 industrial firms. In fact, he presents a model in which he argues that such results are to be expected.

In summary, empirical evidence of FDI spillovers on Chinese domestic firms is mixed, largely because data limitation has hampered the effort to control for the endogenous location of FDI. Thus, while many of the previous studies find positive spillover effects of FDI, the estimates are likely to be biased upward. In fact, the studies that address the endogeneity problem (Hu and Jefferson, 2002; Liu, 2008) do not find positive effects. The message we take from the literature is, therefore, that the evidence of FDI spillovers on domestic firms' productivity in China is inconclusive, at least in the short run.

Another major drawback of the current literature on both direct and spillover effects of FDI in host countries is the lack of research on firm performance measures other than productivity. Firm decisions regarding exports, wage payment, and labor composition, as well as innovation, are also important determinants of both firm growth and overall macroeconomic development. Yet very few studies explore the FDI effects on these aspects of firm development. One of the goals of the current book is to fill this gap in the literature.

1.3. Chinese Manufacturing Firms in 2000–2006

Before turning to the empirical study of how FDI affects firms in China, we first go over some descriptive statistics to present background information on both the patterns of FDI in China between 2000 and 2006 as well as the overall profile of Chinese manufacturing firms during this time period. Here we rely on the data from the manufacturing census for large- and medium-sized firms conducted annually by the China National Bureau of Statistics (described in detail in Chapter 8 and referred to as the NBS manufacturing census hereafter). As the NBS census includes all state-owned firms and firms of other ownership types that have sales over 3 million RMB, the data set essentially includes the big bulk of all firms relevant to our research.

Figure 1.2 presents the foreign capital shares by industry in 2000 and 2006 for two types of FDI in China: foreign capital from the Greater China Area and that from outside the Greater China Area that includes Hong Kong, Macao, and Taiwan (referred as HMT and FRN, respectively, henceforth). The HMT and FRN shares for 2000 and 2006 are shown in the figure for each of the two-digit manufacturing industries based on the China Industry Codes of 2002 (CIC or GB2002).

The first pattern emerging from the figure is that FDI into China continued to grow during 2000–2006 in most sectors, although there is variation between different types of FDI. We can see that during this time period while FRN increased for all industries, HMT did not increase or actually

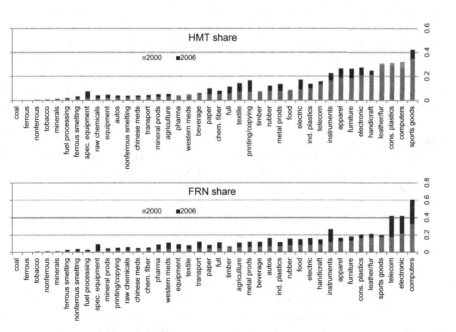

Figure 1.2   FRN and HMT shares in 2000 and 2006.

declined in food manufacturing, leather and fur, timber processing, pharmaceuticals (and in particular western medicine), consumer plastics, and computers. On average FRN share more than doubled while HMT share almost doubled between 2000 and 2006. This indicates that during this time period China has continued to diversify and further globalize the sources of its FDI inflow.

Furthermore, the industries with high FDI presence (both HMT and FRN) at the beginning of the period include sports goods, leather and fur, apparel, furniture, handicraft, and consumer plastics, all labor-intensive sectors that are export-oriented. Computer and electronics industries also had a high presence of FDI. Although these sectors are more capital-intensive, the value added in China is still mainly attributable to labor. On the other hand, the industries where the fastest growth in FDI is observed include computer, electronics, telecommunication, instruments, transportation equipment, automobile, special equipment, and Western medicine. These are all capital-intensive industries and most of the FDI growth is due to increased presence of FRN.

The substantial change in FDI presence over time is important for our analysis, because due to the control of firm fixed effects, the identification of FDI effects in most of our empirical analysis comes from variation in FDI presence over time. The above patterns are also consistent with the government FDI policy changes in recent years that encouraged more investment in capital-intensive industries. In addition, the FDI policies have become more transparent and uniform and thus make it more feasible for capital to come from outside the Greater China Area. In contrast, in industries such as coal, ferrous and nonferrous metals, tobacco, and minerals, the share of both HMT and FRN is negligible both at the beginning and at the end of our sample period; these industries still remain monopolized by state-owned firms.

Tables 1.1 and 1.2 present summary statistics by year for the key features of Chinese manufacturing firms covered in the NBS census, where the top section in Tables 1.1 corresponds to the full sample of firms, while the bottom section of Tables 1.1 and the sections in Tables 1.2 correspond to the domestic firm sample, the HMT firm sample, and the FRN firm sample, respectively. We will first describe the overall dynamics observed and then discuss differences across various firm samples.

The typical size of Chinese firms has generally increased over the 2000–2006 period in terms of real output, but has dropped in employment. The average level of fixed assets also has increased over time, but at a much slower pace than output. Combined together, these patterns imply an upward trend in both labor productivity and capital intensity in Chinese firms during this time period. Along the same line, the ratios of exports to

Table 1.1 Means of key variables.

Year	2000	2001	2002	2003	2004	2005	2006
Means for full sample							
Number of firms	132795	137114	145036	158081	239051	234960	266120
Real output	1045.30	1092.82	1190.80	1393.51	1790.70	2287.80	2752.14
Real capital	893.96	1044.73	1030.84	959.85	1021.91	1140.12	1287.02
Real throughput	603.53	619.72	703.29	845.47	1110.67	1497.61	1798.17
Employees	333.84	308.41	296.60	285.08	229.15	241.36	230.25
Firm age (years)	20.93	18.41	17.24	15.71	12.71	12.61	12.21
Exports/output	15.16%	16.47%	17.45%	19.62%	23.49%	22.84%	23.46%
New product output/output	6.08%	6.12%	6.22%	5.70%	N.A.	6.59%	7.01%
Real wage	8.92	10.40	11.13	12.13	13.85	15.46	17.36
Leverage	66.08%	63.96%	62.50%	61.05%	61.17%	59.23%	58.64%
State share	41.98%	35.94%	30.66%	24.77%	18.84%	15.32%	12.87%
FRN share	5.02%	5.98%	6.71%	7.74%	9.30%	11.04%	11.78%
HMT share	6.19%	7.26%	7.85%	9.22%	11.50%	11.18%	11.75%
Means for domestic firms							
Number of firms	109387	111776	117936	127979	191651	188571	215337
Real output	1097.17	1124.31	1213.56	1402.41	1860.38	2198.30	2668.96
Real capital	1001.72	1152.64	1138.28	1111.18	1247.33	1359.63	1592.91
Real throughput	595.62	596.26	672.38	785.60	1070.26	1306.27	1579.82
Employees	324.16	294.78	281.04	263.57	205.79	211.46	197.26
Firm age (years)	23.30	20.74	19.38	17.62	14.46	14.04	13.60
Exports/output	8.69%	9.24%	9.78%	10.50%	11.63%	11.27%	11.34%
New product output/output	5.62%	5.79%	6.18%	5.61%	N.A.	6.42%	6.50%
Real wage	8.06	9.63	10.20	11.27	13.05	14.37	16.14
Leverage	68.22%	66.14%	64.51%	62.94%	62.94%	60.90%	60.28%
State share	48.42%	42.53%	36.51%	30.41%	24.41%	19.96%	16.96%

All means, except for number of firms and employees, are weighted by number of employees. See Chapter 8 for definitions.

sales and of new product output to total output have both increased, and so have real wages on average. So over time, the typical Chinese manufacturing firm is more productive, more capital-intensive, more innovative, exports more, and pays higher wages. The leverage ratio (or the debt/equity ratio) has also dropped continuously over time, suggesting better financial conditions.

As the Chinese economy grows over time, the number of large- and medium-sized firms has also been increasing during our sample period. As 2004 is a census year when all firms were surveyed, the sample size increased dramatically in that year. A seemingly paradoxical pattern is the decreasing firm age over time. The reason is most likely the large number of new entrants into the large- and medium-sized manufacturing firm census. Note that these are not necessarily new firms. They may either be firms that

Table 1.2   Means of key variables: HMT and FRN firms.

Year	2000	2001	2002	2003	2004	2005	2006
Means for firms with HMT share							
Number of firms	13182	14282	14498	16059	25320	23009	24840
Real output	744.08	781.60	913.70	920.20	1045.68	2595.01	1277.72
Real capital	353.78	597.88	619.20	451.84	417.48	478.31	481.81
Real throughput	576.57	566.29	643.86	668.88	754.37	2198.22	897.55
Employees	367.41	355.63	369.80	373.69	327.22	359.09	372.62
Firm age (years)	11.11	10.23	10.96	9.80	8.38	8.70	8.91
Exports/output	44.05%	44.85%	44.84%	50.05%	56.67%	53.60%	54.59%
New product output/output	7.16%	6.24%	5.34%	4.96%	N.A.	6.10%	6.97%
Real wage	11.40	12.04	12.69	13.11	15.17	15.90	18.00
Leverage	57.16%	55.70%	55.67%	54.88%	56.38%	54.90%	54.61%
State share	13.70%	11.60%	10.96%	6.91%	3.48%	3.25%	2.93%
FRN share	2.05%	1.84%	1.65%	1.45%	0.94%	0.93%	1.07%
HMT share	56.66%	60.43%	63.00%	69.22%	76.02%	76.72%	77.82%
Means for firms with FRN share							
Number of firms	10628	11500	13059	14460	22549	23803	26405
Real output	1145.50	1318.64	1568.26	1948.51	2380.42	2578.06	4652.36
Real capital	630.30	765.30	1055.53	713.12	606.00	881.57	848.68
Real throughput	862.21	946.56	1113.76	1465.13	1799.62	1787.51	3642.15
Employees	426.09	411.55	388.00	398.05	327.91	376.21	379.07
Firm age (years)	12.40	10.55	10.02	10.54	8.30	9.87	9.45
Exports/output	36.80%	38.16%	40.95%	43.01%	50.47%	47.10%	47.12%
New product output/output	10.14%	9.40%	8.10%	7.74%	N.A.	8.30%	9.80%
Real wage	13.49	14.28	16.08	16.50	16.87	20.15	22.17
Leverage	58.08%	57.08%	55.62%	56.05%	56.70%	55.68%	55.27%
State share	20.23%	15.15%	13.49%	10.01%	6.12%	5.78%	4.85%
FRN share	49.16%	53.40%	57.00%	60.57%	68.92%	69.93%	72.10%
HMT share	1.55%	1.48%	1.49%	1.23%	0.91%	0.78%	0.92%

All means, except for number of firms and employees, are weighted by number of employees. See Chapter 8 for definitions.

have newly exceeded the threshold level and have thus been newly included into the survey or firms that changed names and thus registration numbers when going through restructuring.

The most important change during the time period is with regard to the ownership structure of Chinese firms. The share owned by the state has dropped dramatically from 42% to 13%, while both HMT and FRN shares have doubled, from 6% to 12%, and from 5% to 12%, respectively. In terms of firm number in each sample, it has doubled for all three types of firms between 2000 and 2006.

A comparison between domestic firms and foreign-invested firms highlights the following patterns: First of all, Chinese domestic firms are the least efficient in using capital and have become increasingly so from 2000 to 2006. Domestic firms are the largest on average in terms of asset level, followed by FRN firms, and then HMT firms; but the average sales of domestic firms falls behind those of FRN firms, and HMT firms again rank third. In terms of average size of employment, FRN firms are the largest during this time period, followed by the HMT firms, with the level for both groups largely remaining constant. On the Contrary, the employment of a typical domestic firm in our sample is the smallest during the time period and has also shown a substantial decrease (of over 40%) at the same time.

Because the NBS census mainly captures the large- and medium-sized firms in China, these numbers indicate that the domestic Chinese firms have become increasingly more capital-intensive over time, and by now they are even more capital-intensive than foreign-invested firms. In particular, a lot more capital has been invested into the large- and medium-sized domestic manufacturing firms, while their employment has continued to shrink. While the 150% output growth of the domestic firms during 2000–2006 is impressive, their average asset level has grown by 60%. In contrast, the FRN firms have grown by 35% in asset level, but have increased their output by 220%. These numbers, therefore, indicate the inefficiency of capital usage in Chinese domestic firms, as compared to foreign-invested firms. This is also consistent with the pattern that domestic firms in our sample have substantially higher leverage ratios than foreign-invested firms throughout the time period.

Moreover, foreign-invested firms tend to engage more in exporting and innovation. Both HMT firms and other foreign firms have substantially higher export-to-sales ratios than domestic firms. In addition, firms with foreign investment from sources other than HMT tend to have a higher percentage of sales made up of new products, although HMT-invested firms are not substantially different from domestic firms in this respect. Over time, the different groups also show different trends of change. Domestic firms have become more innovative, while the tendency of foreign-invested firms to innovate has not changed much. In contrast, it is the HMT firms and FRN firms that have seen higher growth in the share of exports in total sales, although all firms have become more involved in the overseas market.

These differences between domestic and foreign firms confirm some of the conventional beliefs, challenge others, and leave still others untested. In particular, foreign firms are more internationally-oriented and more technologically innovative. But domestic firms in our sample are the ones that have higher capital intensity. In addition, we observe that domestic firms are gradually narrowing the gap with foreign firms in their tendency to engage in innovation, but the gap between export intensity seems to be growing wider over time. Finally, it is not clear from the summary statistics how the productivity of foreign-invested firms compares to that of domestic firms. Given the multiple factors at work in determining a firm's productivity, such a comparison will require a much more careful analysis, as presented in the next chapter.

1.4. Outline of Book

A few inferences can be made based on the data and facts discussed above: First, FDI has continued to flow into China and we expect this trend to persist in the foreseeable future. Second, over time, FDI will be spread more evenly to more geographic regions in China and enter into a wider range of industries. As a result, it is as important as ever to understand the effects of FDI on the Chinese economy. This volume makes a contribution toward this goal.

Another reason for conducting the current project has been pointed out in the literature review section. The existing studies on FDI effects in China have several drawbacks. First of all, most studies limit their research to total factor productivity or labor productivity. Second, even for studies on TFP, different papers have produced very different results, leading to confusing conclusions. In particular, among studies that find positive FDI spillovers on TFP, many suffer from methodological flaws that lead to upward biases in the estimates or downward-biased standard errors.

In response to the lack of studies on alternative firm performance measures, the current book will explores various aspects of FDI effects, including TFP, wages, and labor composition, exports, as well as new product sales and innovation activity. To address the issues related to methodological difficulties, we will adopt the state-of-the-art econometric methods to conduct more disaggregated studies using firm-level data. In addition, we always cluster the estimated standard errors at the appropriate aggregate level to avoid the downward bias.

While a firm-level panel data-set is necessary for the possibility of solving the aggregation bias and the endogeneity problem (or selection bias), the disaggregated feature of the current book is important for an additional reason. We take seriously the argument made by both Beata Javorcik and Ted Moran that the research focus now should be shifted from reaching generalized conclusions about FDI spillovers to studying the specific conditions under which positive spillovers actually occur (Javorcik, 2008; Moran, 2006). Thus we will explore differences in the effects of FDI along four dimensions that require disaggregated treatment, because such disaggregation is important for a better understanding of the specific conditions that help induce or hinder the positive FDI effects in the host country.

First dimension: We separate FDI into China between two categories, FDI originating from Hong Kong, Macao, and Taiwan (referred to as HMT FDI henceforth) and FDI coming from the other foreign origins (referred to as FRN FDI henceforth). As the HMT region has only recently undergone the industrialization process, which mainland China is currently experiencing, FDI originating from this region is potentially more accessible in the technology it captures. In addition, as the region is both geographically and culturally proximate to China, the cultural and linguistic obstacles in the transfer of technologies and managerial expertise are presumably easier to overcome. In contrast, FDI from other source regions mostly captures much more advanced technologies and uses management styles much different from the conventional ones seen in Chinese firms. The larger technological gap may provide more potential for learning and thus more positive spillovers in domestic Chinese firms. The big cultural differences, on the other hand, may hinder the technology transfer process. Thus, by comparing the different effects of these two types of FDI, we can help shed light on the conditions that enhance or hamper FDI spillovers in the host country.

Second dimension: We study FDI effects by industry, allowing the exploration of specific sectoral conditions that nurture or deter FDI spillovers. As industries both differ in their technological characteristics and face varied regulatory environments, a comparison of how FDI presence affects domestic firms along the sectoral dimension will provide the opportunity to explore what conditions determine the existence and direction of FDI effects. To achieve this goal, we study FDI spillovers on domestic firms in individual two-digit CIC (China Industry Code 2002) industries separately.

Third dimension: We study how domestic firms of different ownership types respond to the presence of FDI differently. State-owned enterprises (SOEs) and private firms in China differ in many aspects, and most of these differences are due to the different regulatory and institutional environments they face. Not legally recognized until the 1980s, Chinese private firms continue to face weak property rights protection, limited access to finance, as well as various entry barriers in many sectors. They also tend to be much younger, smaller, and more labor-intensive than their SOE counterparts, and mainly concentrate in highly competitive industries such as apparel, footwear, consumer electronics, and so on. These features thus may make private firms the more likely prey of their foreign competitors, and thus they may experience negative impacts from FDI presence with a higher likelihood as compared to SOEs. On the other hand, private firms are much more profit-driven and much more nimble, which help predict a better chance of Chinese private firms learning from foreign-invested firms close by, either through demonstration effects or competition effects, and thus enjoying positive FDI spillovers.

Fourth dimension: We study not only effects of FDI presence on domestic firms in the same industry and location (horizontal spillover effects), but also the effects of FDI presence in related industries in the same location (vertical spillover effects). To study the vertical spillover effects, the measure for FDI presence in related industries is constructed using China's input–output table. For FDI presence in a different sector, competition effects may be mitigated yet demonstration effects can still work through formal contracting relationships and informal interactions. Thus, vertical spillovers are more likely to be positive. As Javorcik (2004) demonstrated, vertical spillover effects of FDI may differ dramatically and could be more important compared to horizontal spillover effects.

Another important feature of the current book is that we also study the *direct* FDI effects on the target firms in the host country. We argue that in order to evaluate the spillover effects of FDI on domestic firms, it is crucial that we know how foreign-invested firms behave in the host country. Although the descriptive statistics discussed above provide some information on how foreign firms compare to domestic firms, we still need to explore these patterns more carefully using econometric methods to control for other confounding factors. For example, in order to test the conventional belief that foreign firms are more productive than domestic firms, we will need to estimate TFP and control for endogeneity of FDI, tasks that turn out to be anything but straightforward.

We now outline the structure of the book, followed by a brief summary of the main findings in each chapter. Chapter 2 presents our analysis of how foreign investment affects the target firms, i.e., the foreign-invested firms in China, while FDI spillover effects are studied in Chapters 3 through 6. Specifically, the FDI spillovers on TFP, wages, labor composition, exports, and new product sales and innovation activity of domestic firms are explored in Chapters 3, 4, 5, and 6, respectively.

The main analysis starts in Chapter 2, where we find that FDI from regions outside the Greater China Area tends to increase the total factor productivity of its target firms, while FDI from within the area has ambiguous effects on the TFP of the target firms. There is supporting evidence that the higher transaction costs in the initial acquisition process of HMT investment may be an explanation for the different effects.

The analysis of FDI effects on wages based on the NBS census data set shows that both FRN and HMT investment increases the average wage in target firms, with smaller effects for HMT. Yet the magnitude of the effects is surprisingly small at first sight (an increase from 0% to 100% in foreign share implies an increase in wage by only 4–5%). There are two potential explanations for the small effect on wages: one is the inclusion of firm fixed effects in the estimation, which captures the cross-firm part of the wage differential; the other explanation is the potential differential FDI effects on wages of different categories of labor. Indeed, when the World Bank firm survey of 2000 is used, we find that foreign firms pay significantly more to their engineers and managers, but not to their production workers. As the vast majority of employees are production workers, this may explain the small positive effect of FDI on the average wage in foreign-invested firms. In addition, we find that foreign firms hire younger employees in all categories and better qualified managers (measured by education and foreign experience).

The third direct effect studied in Chapter 2 is the impact of FDI on firm exports. Investment coming from the HMT region tends to have positive effects on target firms' exports on average, while that from other parts of the world has insignificant overall effects on the exports of their target firms. These results suggest that FDI from different origins may be driven by different motives for investing in China. While HMT investment may be seeking an export platform, FRN capital may be motivated by access to the Chinese market gained through the investment. Chapter 2 ends with a discussion of the direct effects of FDI on the target firms's new product development, where no significant differences are found between the probability of new product introduction between foreign-invested firms and domestic firms.

Thus, in Chapter 2 we show that foreign-invested firms tend to be more productive, with FRN-invested firms having a greater advantage. All foreign-invested firms pay higher wages to their engineers and managers, but not necessarily to their production workers. Furthermore, firms with HMT investment (but not FRN investment) also tend to export more of their outputs. Finally, firms with foreign investment are not more likely to have introduced new products, regardless of the country origin of foreign investment.

Chapter 3 is the first chapter to explore spillover effects of FDI presence, where TFP is the performance measure of interest. We find that there are no overall significant horizontal spillover effects of FDI on TFP of domestic firms. However, significant positive horizontal spillovers are observed for private firms as a whole, and there are more significant positive horizontal spillovers of FDI from outside the Greater China Area than of that from within the region. We also study two kinds of vertical spillovers: spillover effects of downstream FDI (or backward linkages) and those of upstream FDI (or forward linkages). For backward linkages, we find no significant overall effects for the full sample of firms. Yet positive effects are found for private firms of downstream FDI both from within and outside the Greater China Area. In particular, these positive effects are larger in size than the horizontal spillovers. In contrast, SOEs suffer significant negative effects from the presence of FDI from outside the Greater China Area in downstream industries. The patterns observed for forward linkages are very similar. We view these findings as additional evidence that private firms are more efficient and more competitive than SOEs.

In Chapter 4 we explore the spillover effects of FDI on wages and labor quality and find that the spillover effects vary along two dimensions. First of all, FDI presence significantly drives up the wages for managers and engineers in domestic firms located nearby, but not the wages for production workers. In addition, private domestic firms raise their wages for managers and engineers in the presence of foreign-invested firms, while SOEs are not significantly affected in these wages. We also find that FDI presence affects labor quality: managers hired by private domestic firms tend to have more foreign experience when FDI is present, yet there is some evidence of quality deterioration for managers employed by SOEs. Put together, these findings suggest that foreign-invested firms impose real competition to Chinese domestic firms in the labor market of skilled workers, thus driving up their wages. Furthermore, the constraints faced by Chinese SOEs may have hampered their ability to compete with foreign firms in the labor market.

The spillover effects of FDI on exports are studied in Chapter 5. While HMT investment is found to have no overall significant effects on same-industry domestic firms' exporting behaviors, FRN investment is shown to have negative and significant effects on the ratio between exports and total sales in domestic firms in the same industry, in particular for private firms. Very similar results are obtained for vertical spillover effects, be they through backward linkages or forward linkages. We interpret these results as reflecting the combined effects of the following mechanisms through which FDI impacts domestic firms: (1) the technological and managerial spillovers that increases the competitiveness of domestic firms' output on the international market; (2) the competition between foreign-invested firms and domestic firms on the export market that pushes domestic firms' output away from exports; and, (3) the supplier and client relationships established between foreign and domestic firms that pull domestic firms' output toward domestic market. The evidence suggests that FDI from regions outside the Greater China Area are more likely to engage domestic firms in their supply chains within China.

Chapter 6 studies the spillover effects of FDI on the innovation behaviors of domestic firms, arguably the most important impact of FDI on the Chinese economy in the long run. The patterns observed, however, suggest a rather grim view of how FDI influences the innovation activity of Chinese indigenous firms. Findings based on the NBS census show that FDI presence significantly lowers the probability of having new product sales in domestic firms, whether FDI is found in the same industry, in downstream industries, or in upstream industries. In addition, the negative effects hold regardless of where the foreign capital comes from. Results from the World Bank data analysis give a somewhat positive picture, where some domestic private firms increase their likelihood of new product introduction. However, these results also indicate that the new products introduced tend to be imitations rather than authentic innovations. Three potential reasons for the lack of positive effects include weak IP protection in China, the greater integration of domestic firms into the global supply chains led by foreign firms that use mature technologies, and potentially the short time span of our data.

Some general conclusions are provided in Chapter 7, where we summarize the findings of each chapter and suggest directions for future research on FDI effects in China. Chapter 8 includes the detailed discussion of the data sets we use as well as the estimation methodologies and specifications adopted in the individual chapters. Finally, while each chapter is an integral part of the whole book, all individual chapters (except Chapter 8) can also be read independently, depending on the interest of the reader.

Chapter 2

Effects of FDI on Target Firms

We begin our analysis of FDI effects with the most obvious question: What are the effects of FDI on the productivity, wages, export activity, and innovation of the target firms? Yet this question is also very difficult because of endogeneity of foreign investment. Simply finding positive correlation between productivity and foreign ownership share, for example, does not indicate causal effect of foreign share — it is just as likely that foreign investors pick the most productive firms as their investment targets. This problem is most prominent in the analysis of productivity, which is why we take special care in addressing it, using both firm fixed effects and propensity score matching. In the analysis of wages we use firm fixed effects and also study in depth employee quality and composition, while in the analysis of export activity and innovation we control for firm fixed effects.[1]

2.1. Effects of FDI on Total Factor Productivity of Target Firms

Our first interest is in the FDI effect on total factor productivity (TFP) of target firms. It is worth mentioning that estimating TFP is not a straightforward task, although a number of approaches have been developed in the industrial organization literature. The main problems that need to be addressed are the endogeneity of inputs and the persistence of variable values. We use dynamic system GMM with firm fixed effects to estimate the production function by industry, which has become the state-of-the-art approach in the literature. The dynamic system GMM uses lagged values of the right-hand side variables as instruments and allows for lagged dependent variable to be included among the regressors, thus addressing both problems — endogeneity and persistence. Many recent papers that analyze the firm-level panel data also use this method, which allows for comparisons.

---

[1]Parts of the text in Section 2 of this chapter appeared in Hale and Long (forthcoming).

Technical details of the dynamic system GMM approach as well as the measures of foreign share are presented in Chapter 8. The data set used for our analysis is the NBS manufacturing census, the detailed description of which is also included in Chapter 8. Because this data set has a panel structure, we are able to estimate our regressions controlling for firm fixed effects. As firm fixed effects absorb all time-invariant differences across firms, therefore the coefficients on foreign shares are identified by variations in foreign ownership shares in firms over time. In order to control for business cycle fluctuations, we also include year-fixed effects in the regressions.

Production processes are very heterogeneous across manufacturing sectors. Accordingly, we mainly conduct our analysis separately for each two-digit industry. We also report the results of our regressions for the full sample of firms, in which case we interact variables measuring inputs: labor, capital, and intermediate inputs, with two-digit industry dummies. See Chapter 8 for detailed description of the estimation method and specifications.

Our data allow us to distinguish between foreign investment from the Greater China Area (Hong Kong, Macao, and Taiwan), which we denote HMT, and from the rest of the world, which we denote FRN. We think it useful to measure the share of ownership by these groups of investors separately for three reasons. First of all, some of the foreign investment from HMT may be in fact domestic investment by firms registered outside the mainland in order to take advantage of tax incentives, a phenomenon referred to in the literature as round-tripping, which is much less likely for investment from the rest of the world. Moreover, technological differences are likely to be smaller between mainland and HMT firms and therefore there is less potential for productivity improvement both in the target firm and in domestic firms. On the other hand, compared to foreign capital from other places, investors from the HMT region may be more familiar with the business culture in China, which may help facilitate the technological and managerial spillovers to domestic firms. For these reasons we include in our regressions two separate measures of foreign share of capital, one for HMT investors and one for FRN investors, both of which we lag by one year in the regression analysis.

The results from system GMM estimations are reported in Table 2.1, where the dependent variable is logarithm of real output of the firm (see Chapter 8 for the detailed description of the method). In the interest of space we only report the coefficients on HMT and FRN shares along with regression diagnostic statistics and do not report the coefficients on lagged output, capital, labor, intermediate inputs, and year dummies. The same

Table 2.1   Effects of FDI on productivity of target firms: Full sample.

Sector	HMT share		FRN share		AR(2)	CRS	N	N_g	j
Full Sample	−0.006	(0.037)	0.335***	(0.041)	0.823	0.983	782297	286792	2433
Ferrous Metals	−2.059	(1.573)	−1.967	(3.757)	0.396	0.486	4711	2146	93
Nonferr. Metals	−0.729*	(0.426)	−0.915	(0.676)	0.649	0.319	4358	1810	93
Nonmetals	1.359	(0.857)	0.468	(1.023)	0.357	0.674	7007	2878	93
Agroproducts	−0.741**	(0.354)	0.612**	(0.295)	0.692	0.019	48868	18862	93
Food	−0.519*	(0.313)	0.441	(0.330)	0.130	0.204	18042	6599	93
Beverage	−0.154	(0.252)	−0.424*	(0.252)	0.980	0.057	13934	4870	93
Textiles	−0.036	(0.161)	1.320***	(0.213)	0.053	0.199	68701	25366	93
Apparel	0.051	(0.116)	0.381***	(0.123)	0.360	0.335	39056	14087	93
Leather/Fur	−0.144	(0.118)	−0.002	(0.135)	0.353	0.791	19185	7077	93
Timber	−0.284	(0.225)	−0.389*	(0.232)	0.311	0.724	14747	6289	93
Furniture	−0.154	(0.132)	−0.046	(0.164)	0.555	0.789	8669	3343	93
Paper	0.108	(0.174)	0.253	(0.212)	0.929	0.764	25646	8937	93
Printing	0.209	(0.267)	0.861*	(0.477)	0.425	0.832	17838	5927	93
Sports Goods	−0.013	(0.069)	0.050	(0.102)	0.146	0.001	10228	3668	93
Fuel Processing	1.086**	(0.521)	0.399	(0.396)	0.583	0.010	5441	2148	93
Raw Chemicals	0.130	(0.162)	0.463***	(0.176)	0.472	0.245	58191	20672	93
Pharmaceutical	−0.371	(0.409)	−0.445	(0.287)	0.358	0.180	17969	5882	93
Chemical Fiber	0.002	(0.276)	0.467	(0.342)	0.533	0.589	3325	1272	93
Rubber Prods.	−0.158	(0.226)	0.095	(0.299)	0.574	0.617	8429	3033	93
Ind. Plastics	−0.070	(0.219)	−0.093	(0.215)	0.515	0.382	18355	7285	93
Cons. Plastics	−0.032	(0.073)	−0.060	(0.090)	0.637	0.114	14818	6119	93
Mineral Prods.	−0.570	(0.457)	1.362**	(0.547)	0.916	0.068	72773	25139	93
Ferr. Smelting	−0.028	(0.377)	0.452	(0.469)	0.797	0.603	17330	7054	93
Nonferr. Smelt.	0.104	(0.503)	0.297	(0.496)	0.217	0.786	12160	4827	93
Metal Prods.	−0.503**	(0.223)	−0.134	(0.275)	0.163	0.479	36754	14229	93
Equipment	0.949***	(0.219)	1.306***	(0.222)	0.360	0.000	54060	20057	93
Spec. Equipment	1.049***	(0.236)	1.265***	(0.267)	0.527	0.001	27539	10445	93
Transport	−0.500	(0.409)	1.084***	(0.288)	0.633	0.009	35427	12503	93
Electric Eq.	−0.191	(0.134)	0.015	(0.175)	0.303	0.049	43653	15693	93
Electronics	−0.520**	(0.238)	0.705***	(0.230)	0.616	0.001	24788	8812	93
Instruments	0.026	(0.195)	0.533***	(0.177)	0.242	0.305	9949	3567	93
Handicraft	0.057	(0.137)	0.325	(0.200)	0.460	0.908	15196	5717	93

Dependent variable is log of output. Estimated using system GMM. Coefficients for the constant, lagged log of output, log of capital, log of labor, log of intermediate inputs, and year dummies are not displayed for presentation purposes. Full sample regression includes log of capital, log of labor, and log of intermediate inputs interacted with CIC2 industry codes. Robust standard errors in parentheses, $^*p < 0.10$, $^{**}p < 0.05$, $^{***}p < 0.01$. AR(2) and CRS present p-values for AR(2) and constant return to scale tests, respectively. N is the number of observations, while N_g is the number of firms, and j is the number of instruments.

HMT share   FRN share

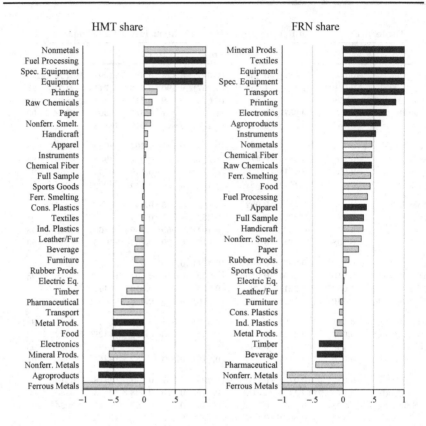

Figure 2.1 Effects of FDI on productivity of target firms: Full sample.
Note: Dark bars represent coefficients that are statistically significant at least at 10%
level.

coefficients on HMT and FRN shares are reported in Figure 2.1 with industries ordered by the size of the coefficient and where darker bars indicate
statistical significance of the coefficients (at 10% significance level). The
magnitudes of the coefficients are easily interpreted. If multiplied by 100
they show by how many percentage points the TFP of the firm would
increase if foreign share in that firm increases from 0% to 100%.

For FRN shares, our findings are largely in line with the common belief
that foreign investment embodies higher productivity, as the direct effect
of FRN shares on target firms' TFP is positive and significant for the full
sample of firms. The magnitude of the full sample effect of FRN is rather
large — an increase in foreign share from 0% to 100% would increase the
productivity of an average firm by 33.5%. Yet, for HMT shares, there is no

significant overall effect of foreign investment on the target firms' productivity, either positive or negative.

At the more disaggregated level, a more mixed picture emerges: We can see that for the two-digit-CIC sectors coefficients on FRN share are predominantly positive, but there are as many positive as there are negative coefficients on HMT share. Consequently, the coefficient for the full sample of firms is not statistically different from zero for HMT share. The different results between FRN and HMT are also consistent with previous findings, which also tend to find more positive effects of investment from outside of the Greater China region than that from within (see Ge and Chen, 2008; Ng and Tuan, 2005).

As we can vividly see from Figure 2.1, the effects vary widely across industries. The effect of foreign investment from outside Greater China Area, FRN, is the highest for textiles, mineral products, equipment, and transportation industries. In these industries an increase in FRN share from 0% to 100% would more than double the TFP. Similarly, foreign investment from the Greater China region, HMT, also has large and significant positive effects on the TFP in fuel processing and equipment. On the other hand, there was no statistically significant direct effect at all in other industries from either FRN or HMT. The effect is, moreover, significantly negative for firms with HMT investment in agroproducts, nonferrous metals, metal products, food, and electronics industries and for FRN firms in timber and beverage industries. It is especially interesting that firms with FRN investment in electronics and agroproducts industries tend to have significantly higher productivity, while those with HMT investment in these same industries tend to have lower productivity. Such variations across industries highlight the importance of disaggregated studies.

In order to see whether the above results are driven by initial foreign acquisition or whether the amount of foreign investment is also important, we limit our sample to firms that have nonzero foreign share, either from within or from outside the Greater China Area, and repeat the above analysis. The results are reported in Table 2.2 and Figure 2.2. The overall picture remains similar with respect to FRN, but changes quite a bit with respect to HMT — while initial foreign investment by an HMT firm lowers productivity for as many industry as it increases productivity, an increase in HMT share for firms that already had some foreign share is clearly associated with an increase in productivity. This result is driven by the fact that negative coefficients that were significant above became smaller and lost their significance, while some coefficients that were not significant now became positive and significant. The effect of HMT on firms producing equipment (and special equipment) is positive in both cases but smaller in magnitude when we exclude observations for domestic firms. The effects of FRN are

Table 2.2 Effects of FDI on productivity of target firms: Foreign firms.

Sector	HMT share		FRN share		AR(2)	CRS	N	N_g	j
Full Sample	0.315	(0.201)	0.548	(0.526)	0.274	0.966	160980	54911	2378
Ferrous Metals	0.106	(4.327)	0.211	(3.805)	0.418	0.977	54	23	54
Nonferr. Metals	0.769	(1.410)	1.007*	(0.555)	0.945	0.921	78	39	57
Nonmetals	0.196	(2.780)	−0.025	(2.896)	0.837	0.830	292	118	93
Agroproducts	0.155	(0.179)	0.450**	(0.191)	0.192	0.116	6803	2238	93
Food	0.356	(0.237)	0.721***	(0.221)	0.068	0.037	4170	1353	93
Beverage	0.278	(0.218)	0.362	(0.241)	0.223	0.147	2287	669	93
Textiles	0.361**	(0.144)	0.470***	(0.132)	0.093	0.183	14120	4943	93
Apparel	0.235	(0.162)	0.386**	(0.169)	0.109	0.006	16489	5683	93
Leather/Fur	0.177	(0.118)	0.274**	(0.138)	0.418	0.141	7577	2564	93
Timber	0.033	(0.244)	0.238	(0.236)	0.110	0.738	2654	964	93
Furniture	0.053	(0.164)	0.042	(0.205)	0.652	0.333	2794	979	93
Paper	0.207	(0.180)	0.449**	(0.218)	0.984	0.081	3860	1247	93
Printing	0.223	(0.205)	0.191	(0.236)	0.233	0.055	2280	686	93
Sports Goods	0.041	(0.149)	0.125	(0.183)	0.187	0.005	4718	1572	93
Fuel Processing	−0.037	(0.354)	0.383	(0.265)	0.332	0.135	471	160	93
Raw Chemicals	0.349*	(0.178)	0.427**	(0.171)	0.123	0.027	9211	3039	93
Pharmaceutical	0.430	(0.283)	0.361	(0.273)	0.130	0.005	3064	979	93
Chemical Fiber	0.037	(0.145)	0.070	(0.230)	0.702	0.724	703	266	93
Rubber Prods.	−0.001	(0.129)	0.104	(0.134)	0.476	0.055	1772	598	93
Ind. Plastics	−0.020	(0.124)	0.020	(0.154)	0.697	0.586	4020	1515	93
Cons. Plastics	−0.109	(0.232)	0.027	(0.224)	0.384	0.011	5152	1931	93
Mineral Prods.	−0.085	(0.253)	0.205	(0.281)	0.150	0.941	7792	2564	93
Ferr. Smelting	−0.272	(0.306)	−0.205	(0.311)	0.238	0.525	1242	466	93
Nonferr. Smelt.	0.214	(0.295)	0.268	(0.284)	0.968	0.845	1261	501	93
Metal Prods.	−0.107	(0.208)	0.113	(0.245)	0.783	0.618	7413	2582	93
Equipment	0.452***	(0.114)	0.482***	(0.094)	0.640	0.001	7487	2677	93
Spec. Equipment	0.350**	(0.145)	0.311**	(0.150)	0.985	0.162	4456	1737	93
Transport	0.427	(0.397)	0.923***	(0.302)	0.337	0.008	5973	1998	93
Electric Eq.	0.271**	(0.134)	0.360***	(0.123)	0.893	0.006	9738	3407	93
Electronics	0.558	(0.397)	0.932***	(0.358)	0.466	0.010	12987	4457	93
Instruments	0.590	(0.414)	0.817**	(0.374)	0.882	0.232	3453	1133	93
Handicraft	0.013	(0.167)	0.289	(0.193)	0.155	0.005	5208	1793	93

Dependent variable is log of output. Estimated using system GMM. Coefficients for the constant, lagged log of output, log of capital, log of labor, log of intermediate inputs, and year dummies are not displayed for presentation purposes. Full sample regression includes log of capital, log of labor, and log of intermediate inputs interacted with CIC2 industry codes. Robust standard errors in parentheses, $*p < 0.10$, $**p < 0.05$, $***p < 0.01$. AR(2) and CRS present p-values for AR(2) and constant return to scale tests, respectively. N is the number of observations, while N_g is the number of firms, and j is the number of instruments.

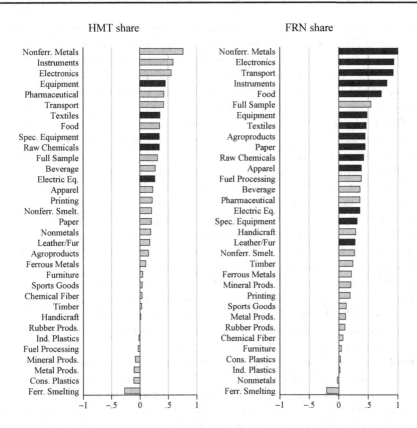

Figure 2.2   Effects of FDI on productivity of target firms: Foreign firms.
Note: Dark bars represent coefficients that are statistically significant at least at 10%
level.

similar to the ones shown above. The coefficient for the full sample is still
positive and is in fact larger in magnitude than for the full sample, but is
no longer statistically significant. The magnitudes of significant coefficients
are now smaller, indicating that an incremental increase in the FRN share
does not have as large an effect on productivity as initial investment.

There are two potential reasons for the differences between results comparing foreign-invested firms and domestic firms and those focusing on
foreign firms with regard to the source of foreign capital. We will begin
with the first set of results (see Table 2.1 and Figure 2.1). On one hand,
the results may reflect the time-varying intrinsic productivity differences
(as firm fixed effects are already controlled for) between firms acquired by
foreign investment from different origins as well as productivity differences

due to the foreign acquisition that change over time. Hence, the more negative effects of HMT-invested firms as compared to those in firms with FRN
investment may indicate the higher ability of investors from outside the
Greater China Area to either pick the "winners" or to improve the productivity of the target firms. On the other hand, to the extent that such
intrinsic differences between foreign-invested firms and domestic firms are
controlled for in the estimation, the less impressive performance of HMT-
invested firms may suggest higher transaction costs during the initial acquisition stage than the FRN-invested firms. Although the closer geographic
and cultural affinity enjoyed by investors from HMT would suggest lower
transaction costs, expenses involved in round-tripping and other kinds of
shadowy deals may as well lead to higher costs.

Combined with the second set of results (see Table 2.2 and Figure 2.2),
the initial transaction costs argument seems more like the better explanation. Because the initial transaction costs is not an issue for firms that
continue to increase foreign shares, both HMT firms and FRN firms enjoy
positive effects in more industries. At the same time, the disappearance of
negative results for the HMT firms is also consistent with the lack of additional costs. If the different results are due to selection, on the other hand,
then the productivity disadvantage in HMT firms should be more persistent. Consequently, these above results suggest that the differential TFP
effects of foreign capital from different regions may be due to the different
transaction costs involved in the initial acquisition process. Paradoxically,
it is foreign capital from the Greater China Area that incurs higher transaction costs in the process, which may explain the lack of significant positive
impact on TFP for such FDI. However, this may not be that surprising
when considering the possibility of round-tripping FDI.

To address the above concern with regard to endogeneity of foreign
direct investment even better, we follow Arnold and Javorcik (2009) and
conduct a difference-in-differences analysis on a matched sample. To do so,
we estimate an auxiliary regression of the probability that a firm has some
foreign investment, the results of which are reported in Table 2.3. From this
regression we construct the propensity score, i.e., the predicted probability
of having foreign investment. We then restrict the sample to firms with
and without foreign investment that have similar propensity scores at some
point in our sample period.

For this sample, we rerun our regression as before, with the results
reported in Table 2.4 and Figure 2.3. The results show that for this matched
sample we find very similar effects of FRN and HMT as for the full sample including all domestic and foreign-invested firms. Coefficients in a few
industries either lose or gain statistical significance, but the overall picture
remains the same. Given that we use system GMM and control for firm fixed

Table 2.3 Predicting foreign acquisition: Probit regression results.

TFP	−0.0474***	(0.00798)
Log(employees)	0.308***	(0.0158)
Log(employees)^2	−0.0130***	(0.00152)
Log(wage)	0.622***	(0.00520)
Capital/labor (1)	0.000719***	(0.0000392)
(1)*exporter	0.0000877*	(0.0000356)
Exporter	1.017***	(0.00552)
SOE	−0.153***	(0.00904)
Investment	−0.664***	(0.0564)
Leverage	−0.00000293***	(0.000000329)
Firm age	0.0278***	(0.00122)
Firm age^2	−0.00159***	(0.0000408)
(1)*Firm age	−0.0000119***	(0.00000275)
Year 2003	−0.124***	(0.00842)
Year 2004	−0.178***	(0.00851)
Year 2005	−0.326***	(0.00818)
Year 2006	−0.401***	(0.00764)
Constant	−3.593***	(0.0433)
N	480983	
Pseudo R^2	0.252	

Dependent variable is binary outcome of a firm becoming acquired by Hong Kong–Macao–Taiwan or other foreign entities. Robust standard errors in parentheses, $^*p < 0.10$, $^{**}p < 0.05$, $^{***}p < 0.01$. All explanatory variables are lagged one period except for age and year fixed effects.

effects, we are fairly confident that these results could be interpreted as causal. In addition, our discussion above comparing the results from the full sample and those from the foreign firm sample suggests that sample selection is less likely to account for the results. Therefore, we are quite comfortable to interpret our results as evidence that firms with foreign investment from outside of the Greater China Area tend to become more productive, while the effects of investment from within the Greater China Area on target firms' TFP are ambiguous on average. For both types of foreign investment, the specific effect for firms will depend on the industry.

2.2. Effects of FDI on Wages and Labor Quality of Target Firms

Next, we study the direct effects of FDI in the labor market. Since foreign investment has a positive effect on productivity, we may expect it to also increase wages in the target firms. In addition, there may be effects on the quality of employees working in firms with foreign investment.

Table 2.4   Effects of FDI on productivity of target firms: Matched sample.

Sector	HMT share		FRN share		AR(2)	CRS	N	N_g	j
Full Sample	−0.016	(0.035)	0.314***	(0.040)	0.868	0.559	702379	215096	2433
Ferrous Metals	−2.835*	(1.649)	−2.975	(5.111)	0.408	0.140	3903	1357	93
Nonferr. Metals	−0.738	(0.457)	−0.721	(0.612)	0.730	0.510	3739	1220	93
Nonmetals	1.513*	(0.887)	−0.034	(1.101)	0.199	0.225	6018	1976	93
Agroproducts	−0.772**	(0.364)	0.696**	(0.317)	0.663	0.565	43413	13691	93
Food	−0.430	(0.317)	0.536	(0.348)	0.126	0.957	16131	4830	93
Beverage	−0.112	(0.283)	−0.035	(0.256)	0.976	0.279	12352	3568	93
Textiles	0.053	(0.140)	1.172***	(0.211)	0.059	0.873	56288	18356	93
Apparel	−0.004	(0.112)	0.296***	(0.114)	0.356	0.061	35713	10835	93
Leather/Fur	−0.186	(0.117)	−0.003	(0.151)	0.413	0.166	17467	5407	93
Timber	−0.214	(0.212)	−0.214	(0.201)	0.307	0.781	12789	4370	93
Furniture	−0.146	(0.135)	−0.110	(0.167)	0.594	0.730	7790	2485	93
Paper	0.231	(0.201)	0.312	(0.239)	0.993	0.979	23531	6942	93
Printing	0.115	(0.240)	0.614	(0.397)	0.366	0.784	15777	4455	93
Sports Goods	0.049	(0.076)	−0.011	(0.111)	0.050	0.007	9424	2804	93
Fuel Processing	1.347***	(0.516)	0.658	(0.410)	0.469	0.082	4791	1521	93
Raw Chemicals	0.038	(0.162)	0.352*	(0.182)	0.380	0.671	52963	15773	93
Pharmaceutical	−0.739**	(0.363)	−0.332	(0.266)	0.486	0.230	16317	4467	93
Chemical Fiber	−0.021	(0.276)	0.412	(0.304)	0.462	0.648	3075	1023	93
Rubber Prods.	−0.289	(0.236)	0.096	(0.322)	0.599	0.385	7662	2318	93
Ind. Plastics	−0.212	(0.181)	0.041	(0.215)	0.548	0.724	16619	5586	93
Cons. Plastics	−0.040	(0.076)	−0.071	(0.090)	0.702	0.061	13321	4638	93
Mineral Prods.	−0.455	(0.426)	1.866***	(0.520)	0.768	0.559	66672	19351	93
Ferr. Smelting	−0.217	(0.338)	0.316	(0.500)	0.768	0.743	15339	5151	93
Nonferr. Smelt.	−0.004	(0.443)	0.202	(0.479)	0.195	0.920	10814	3551	93
Metal Prods.	−0.720**	(0.312)	−0.031	(0.371)	0.132	0.907	33010	10619	93
Equipment	0.875***	(0.208)	1.165***	(0.212)	0.437	0.000	48742	15251	93
Spec. Equipment	0.907***	(0.241)	1.050***	(0.260)	0.278	0.006	24560	7741	93
Transport	−0.285	(0.378)	0.849***	(0.262)	0.379	0.016	31988	9486	93
Electric Eq.	−0.542***	(0.181)	−0.164	(0.241)	0.092	0.343	40400	12246	93
Electronics	−0.427*	(0.223)	0.645***	(0.212)	0.549	0.001	22907	6997	93
Instruments	0.009	(0.182)	0.474***	(0.164)	0.281	0.132	9072	2737	93
Handicraft	0.049	(0.144)	0.342	(0.211)	0.470	0.459	13721	4275	93

Dependent variable is log of output. Estimated using system GMM. Matched sample based on the common support of propensity score. Coefficients for the constant, lagged log of output, log of capital, log of labor, log of intermediate inputs, and year dummies are not displayed for presentation purposes. Full sample regression includes log of capital, log of labor, and log of intermediate inputs interacted with CIC2 industry codes. Robust standard errors in parentheses, $*p < 0.10$, $**p < 0.05$, $***p < 0.01$. AR(2) and CRS present p-values for AR(2) and constant return to scale tests, respectively. N is the number of observations, while N_g is the number of firms, and j is the number of instruments.

HMT share   FRN share

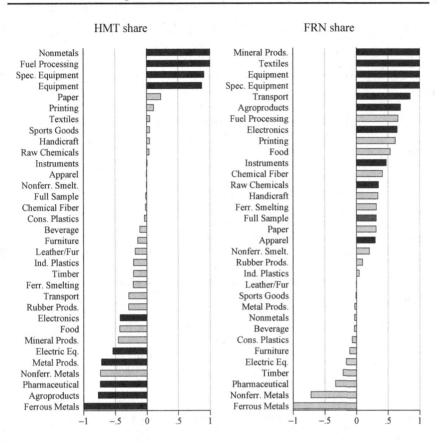

Figure 2.3 Effects of FDI on productivity of target firms: Matched sample.
Note: Dark bars represent coefficients that are statistically significant at least at 10%
level.

To our knowledge, there has been little research on the FDI effects on
labor quality. On the other hand, literature on wages in foreign-invested
enterprises has produced different results for different countries. Aitken,
Harrison, and Lipsey (1996) finds that higher FDI is associated with higher
wages in foreign-invested firms, Conyon, Girma, Thompson, and Wrights
(2002) and Girma and Görg (2007) find some positive effects on unskilled
wages in the UK, and the Lipsey and Sjöholm (2004) study for Indonesia
finds positive effects of FDI on wages. In contrast, Almeida (2007) and Heyman, Sjöholm, and Tingvall (2007) find no effects for Sweden and Portugal,
respectively. In a related paper, Braconier, Norback, and Urban (2005)
study the role of low labor costs in attracting FDI.

Table 2.5 Effects of FDI on wage: Full sample.

	(1)	(2)	(3)	(4)	(5)
HMT share	0.0275***	0.0391***	0.0275***	0.0269***	0.0390***
	(0.00627)	(0.00622)	(0.00628)	(0.00627)	(0.00623)
FRN share	0.0331***	0.0477***	0.0326***	0.0325***	0.0470***
	(0.00655)	(0.00646)	(0.00655)	(0.00655)	(0.00647)
Year 2001	0.0439***	0.0288***	0.0436***	0.0437***	0.0290***
	(0.00222)	(0.00214)	(0.00222)	(0.00222)	(0.00214)
Year 2002	0.101***	0.0799***	0.0996***	0.100***	0.0800***
	(0.00237)	(0.00230)	(0.00238)	(0.00238)	(0.00231)
Year 2003	0.133***	0.113***	0.131***	0.132***	0.113***
	(0.00247)	(0.00242)	(0.00248)	(0.00248)	(0.00242)
Year 2004	0.283***	0.260***	0.281***	0.282***	0.260***
	(0.00241)	(0.00236)	(0.00243)	(0.00242)	(0.00237)
Year 2005	0.383***	0.373***	0.381***	0.382***	0.372***
	(0.00244)	(0.00240)	(0.00247)	(0.00246)	(0.00242)
Year 2006	0.498***	0.495***	0.495***	0.497***	0.495***
	(0.00247)	(0.00243)	(0.00251)	(0.00248)	(0.00246)
Log(employees)		−0.230***			−0.229***
		(0.00243)			(0.00251)
Capital/labor			0.0000408***		0.00000719
			(0.0000115)		(0.00000656)
State share				−0.0162***	0.00229
				(0.00490)	(0.00481)
Constant	1.972***	3.071***	1.970***	1.974***	3.065***
	(0.00210)	(0.0117)	(0.00220)	(0.00222)	(0.0122)
Observations	1231289	1231289	1229078	1231289	1229078
Firms	426978	426978	426231	426978	426231
Overall R^2	0.107	0.0419	0.112	0.109	0.0424

Firm fixed effects regressions. Dependent variable is log of wages. Robust standard errors in parentheses; $^*p < 0.10$, $^{**}p < 0.05$, $^{***}p < 0.01$.

We know of no studies on FDI effects on wages in the Chinese context. To fill in the gap, we first use the NBS census data to test whether foreign-invested firms pay higher wages. Table 2.5 reports the results of the following regression, conducted using the full sample of firms for which data are available in 2000–2006: wages (in logs) is the dependent variable, and the shares of paid-up capital owned by investors from the Greater China Area and from other foreign countries are the main explanatory variables. We see strong positive correlations between foreign share and wages, even after controlling for firm and year fixed effects, firm size (measured in log(number of employees)), capital–labor ratio, and the share of state ownership. We also find firms that hire more employees, with lower capital intensity, and have a larger state share tend to pay lower wages, as we would expect. These control variables are highly correlated and only the size of the firm enters significantly when we include all three of the additional control variables together.

In addition, the effect on wages of FDI from the Greater China Area is not as large as that of investment from other foreign countries, consistent with the previous finding that HMT firms experiencing less productivity increase. Somewhat surprisingly, the magnitudes of the effects are economically meaningful but not very large. At the extreme — an increase in the share of capital owned by the Greater China Area from 0% to 100% would lead to about 4% increase in the average wage of the firm. Likewise, an increase in the share of capital owned by firms from outside of the Greater China Area from 0% to 100% would lead to about 5% increase in the average wage. Because we include firm fixed effects, these results suggest that an increase in the share of foreign capital leads to an increase in the average wage for the target firms. Furthermore, the estimated coefficients may underestimate the total magnitude of the FDI effects on wages, as part of the wage differential may have already been captured in the firm fixed effects.

In the above regression the explanatory variable, foreign share, is continuous, while the sample includes a large number of firms that are fully domestically owned, about 80% of observations. In order to see whether these results are driven by the differences between fully domestic firms and firms with some foreign ownership share or by the differences in the foreign share of the firms that have some foreign share, we repeat our analysis for the subsample of firms that have either positive share of investment from the Greater China Area or from other foreign countries.

The results are reported in Table 2.6. We can see that there is no effect of the share of investment from either the Greater China Area or other countries on wages of firms that have some foreign ownership. Thus, we conclude that wages tend to be higher in the firms with some foreign ownership share, but once there is positive foreign investment, the actual share of foreign investment has no effect on wages.

The NBS manufacturing census data set is extremely comprehensive in its coverage of firms, but it does have one limitation. It does not allow us to differentiate between skilled and unskilled wages, which is very important given the limited supply of skilled labor and the seemingly unlimited supply of unskilled labor in China at least till very recently. The lack of such information also prohibits us from analyzing the effects of foreign investment on labor quality. In order to conduct a more complete analysis of the effects of FDI on wages and labor quality of target firms, we make use of a different data set, the 2001 World Bank Industrial Survey, described

Table 2.6   Effects of FDI on wage: Foreign firms.

	(1)	(2)	(3)	(4)	(5)
HMT share	−0.000758	−0.00656	−0.00124	−0.000935	−0.00554
	(0.0111)	(0.0111)	(0.0111)	(0.0112)	(0.0111)
FRN share	0.00233	−0.00186	0.00137	0.00215	−0.00151
	(0.0111)	(0.0110)	(0.0111)	(0.0111)	(0.0111)
Year 2001	0.0345***	0.0328***	0.0337***	0.0344***	0.0327***
	(0.00467)	(0.00454)	(0.00466)	(0.00467)	(0.00454)
Year 2002	0.0839***	0.0867***	0.0829***	0.0839***	0.0864***
	(0.00481)	(0.00470)	(0.00479)	(0.00481)	(0.00470)
Year 2003	0.118***	0.129***	0.118***	0.118***	0.129***
	(0.00496)	(0.00488)	(0.00494)	(0.00496)	(0.00488)
Year 2004	0.230***	0.250***	0.230***	0.230***	0.249***
	(0.00483)	(0.00479)	(0.00481)	(0.00483)	(0.00479)
Year 2005	0.320***	0.352***	0.319***	0.320***	0.352***
	(0.00487)	(0.00489)	(0.00486)	(0.00488)	(0.00490)
Year 2006	0.444***	0.487***	0.444***	0.444***	0.487***
	(0.00497)	(0.00505)	(0.00495)	(0.00498)	(0.00505)
Log (employees)		−0.212*** (0.00508)			−0.207*** (0.00541)
Capital/labor			0.000114*** (0.0000339)		0.0000336* (0.0000189)
State share				−0.00264 (0.0146)	0.0146 (0.0144)
Constant	2.341***	3.407***	2.327***	2.341***	3.376***
	(0.00871)	(0.0268)	(0.00969)	(0.00881)	(0.0293)
Observations	246882	246404	246882	246404	246882
Firms	79969	79969	79811	79969	79811
Overall R^2	0.0486	0.0791	0.0566	0.0526	0.0566

Dependent variable is log of wages. Firm fixed effects regressions. Foreign sample defined as sample consisting of firms with nonzero Hong Kong–Macao–Taiwan (HMT) and/or other foreign capital. Robust standard errors in parentheses.

in detail in Chapter 8. The survey has detailed information on wages for skilled and unskilled labor, as well as information on various indicators of labor quality. While this data set is cross-sectional and thus does not allow us to fully address the endogeneity problem discussed above, it does allow us to conduct a more nuanced analysis of the relationship between foreign investment and wage as well as quality of labor. The data, however, do not allow us to distinguish the different effects of HMT versus FRN.

Using the World Bank survey data, we explore the direct effects of FDI on wages and labor quality by estimating differences between domestic

Table 2.7 Foreign ownership, wage, and labor quality.

Dependent variable	β (foreign share)	Robust S.e.	Controls	Adj.R^2	N.(obs)
Wage					
Log (average wage)					
Production workers	0.16	(0.12)	log(K/L)	0.06	791
Engineers	0.29**	(0.13)	log(K/L)	0.12	832
Managers	0.50***	(0.11)	log(K/L)	0.15	1075
Production workers	0.14	(0.13)	log(K/L), quality[a]	0.06	776
Engineers	0.24*	(0.13)	log(K/L), quality[a]	0.12	801
Managers	0.36***	(0.12)	log(K/L), quality[a]	0.16	1017
Labor quality					
Avg. age					
Production workers	−2.33***	(0.79)	log(K), firm age	0.33	782
Engineers	−2.32***	(0.76)	log(K), firm age	0.26	837
Managers	−1.63**	(0.70)	log(K), firm age	0.22	1071
Avg. education					
Production workers	0.15	(0.19)	log(K)	0.21	782
Engineers	0.11	(0.17)	log(K)	0.20	839
Managers	0.73***	(0.15)	log(K)	0.28	1074
Avg. foreign experience					
Engineers	0.009	(0.007)	log(K)	0.12	815
Managers	0.12***	(0.033)	log(K)	0.09	1027

*Significant at 10%; **significant at 5%; ***significant at 1%.
[a]Quality controls include average age, average age squared, and average education of the relevant group as well as controls for foreign experience for engineers and managers. Estimated by OLS. City*sector fixed effects included in all regression Sample limited to domestic private and foreign-invested firms.

and foreign firms included in the survey. To abstract from the complexity added by state ownership, we exclude SOEs in the survey sample from our analysis, which are defined as domestic firms with less than 100% of private ownership share. We then analyze the relationship between wages (or labor quality) of a firm and its foreign share of ownership, controlling for city–industry pair fixed effects. The technical details of our analysis are in Chapter 8. Table 2.7 shows the estimated direct effects of FDI on wages and labor quality. As a robustness test, we excluded SOE firms according to their legal status (instead of state shares) and obtained similar results.

The first finding is that, whether or not we control for observed quality of labor, firms with higher shares of foreign ownership pay higher average wages to their engineers and managers. Part of the wage premium is explained by the higher quality of managers, as the coefficient on the foreign share is smaller once we control for observed quality (as captured in age and education), while the rest may be due to unobserved variation in quality not controlled for by age and education. The other finding is the surprising results observed for production workers. Although the point estimate is positive, there is no statistically significant effect of foreign ownership on the average wage of production workers!

In addition, we find that firms with higher shares of foreign ownership tend to hire younger workers of all types, as well as more educated managers who are also more likely to have foreign working experience. Taken together, these results show that foreign-invested firms seek younger employees (note that we condition on firm age), better qualified managers, and are willing to pay higher wages to their engineers and managers, but not to their production workers.

The above effects are substantial in terms of magnitude. Managers in fully foreign owned firms would get paid 51% more than in fully domestic private firms, with 9 percentage points due to their observable quality advantage, while engineers in fully foreign owned firms get on average 30% higher wages compared to fully domestic private firms. Compared to domestic private firms, firms with 100% foreign ownership would hire engineers and production workers that are on average 2.3 years younger. They would also employ managers that are on average 1.6 years younger, have 8.5 more months of education, and are 12 percentage points more likely to have foreign working experience.

Although foreign investment has significant and large positive effects on manager and engineer wages in target firms, the majority of employees in Chinese firms are still unskilled production workers. As shown above, foreign-invested firms do not pay their production workers significantly more than domestic firms. Combined together, these results thus provide another explanation for the relatively small effect of foreign investment on the average wage in target firms (Table 2.5).[2]

2.3. Effects of FDI on Exports of Target Firms

Another commonly believed effect of foreign investment is on the target firm's exports. There are a number of reasons to believe that foreign

---

[2]The other potential explanation discussed previously is the inclusion of firm fixed effects in the average wage estimation, which may have captured part of the wage differential between foreign-invested firms and domestic firms.

investment is likely to facilitate exporting activity of target firms. From the theoretical point of view, firms with higher productivity are more likely to be able to pay the fixed cost of entering export market (Melitz, 2003). Since FDI increases the target firm's productivity, they are also likely to move firms over the cost threshold and make exports profitable for them. A second argument relating FDI to increased export is that exporting requires specific human capital and institutional knowledge that foreign investors can bring to the target firms in China, even if they are not increasing TFP. Finally, in the case of China especially, it may have been the foreign investor's chief goal from the very beginning to turn the target firm into an exporter by taking advantage of domestic cheap labor.

In this section, we test whether the empirical evidence supports the above reasoning. As with total factor productivity, we estimate the effects of foreign investment from Hong Kong, Macao, or Taiwan separately from that of other foreign countries. And similarly, we estimate the effects separately for each industry, controlling for firm and year-fixed effects, using FE regressions. The dependent variable is the ratio between export and total sales, and as additional controls we include firm size (measured as log of number of employees), firm age, and leverage (measured as the ratio between total debt and total asset). In the interest of space we do not report the coefficients on the control variables but only coefficients on foreign shares. As usual, details of the estimation procedure and variable definitions can be found in Chapter 8.

Results are reported in Table 2.8 and Figure 2.4 for the full sample of firms. We find that although the overall effect on export in target firms is positive and significant for HMT investment, this is largely driven by positive effects only in a few industries. The first result is consistent with the argument that the large inflow of FDI into China is mainly driven by the globalization process, in which investors in East Asia move capital from the Greater China Area (where labor cost has risen thanks to earlier export driven growth) to China, which still has the comparative advantage of low labor costs. Since many investors from the Greater China Area rely on cheap labor in China to manufacture products for sales to overseas markets, it is then natural that firms funded by Hong Kong, Macao, and Taiwan capital tend to be largely export-oriented.

Against this background, it is then natural to see where the positive effects of HMT share on exports are observed. Specifically, positive spillovers are found for firms in apparel, nonferrous smelting, metal products, and electric equipment industries. With the exception of nonferrous smelting, these are indeed heavily export-oriented industries, which also tend to be labor-intensive. We also need to point out that the magnitudes of the effects are rather small — an increase in HMT share from 0% to

Table 2.8   Effect of FDI on exports: Full sample.

Sector	HMT share		FRN share		N	N_g	r2_o
Full Sample	0.007*	(0.004)	0.004	(0.004)	734732	276150	0.054
Ferrous Metals	0.001	(0.001)	−0.000	(0.001)	4436	2051	0.002
Nonferr. Metals	−0.006	(0.014)	0.044	(0.080)	4138	1751	0.006
Nonmetals	−0.010	(0.039)	0.073	(0.047)	6488	2740	0.009
Agroproducts	0.000	(0.013)	0.003	(0.015)	45937	18215	0.019
Food	0.016	(0.013)	0.008	(0.011)	17043	6387	0.033
Beverage	−0.010	(0.011)	−0.001	(0.011)	12929	4653	0.001
Textiles	0.004	(0.012)	0.004	(0.013)	66369	24848	0.021
Apparel	0.025*	(0.015)	−0.003	(0.016)	35429	13400	0.054
Leather/Fur	−0.013	(0.022)	−0.020	(0.024)	17613	6787	0.048
Timber	−0.039	(0.030)	−0.045*	(0.027)	13823	6028	0.016
Furniture	0.043	(0.028)	0.024	(0.029)	8106	3222	0.172
Paper	−0.024	(0.016)	−0.012	(0.018)	24473	8663	0.026
Printing	−0.012	(0.016)	0.032	(0.022)	16080	5654	0.018
Sports Goods	0.036	(0.027)	0.014	(0.028)	9514	3570	0.117
Fuel Processing	−0.002	(0.008)	0.002	(0.013)	5161	2075	0.005
Raw Chemicals	0.002	(0.011)	−0.005	(0.010)	55240	19980	0.005
Pharmaceutical	0.017	(0.011)	0.005	(0.011)	16906	5632	0.003
Chemical Fiber	0.025	(0.050)	0.056	(0.042)	3186	1239	0.058
Rubber Prods.	−0.017	(0.035)	−0.001	(0.033)	7945	2924	0.004
Ind. Plastics	0.007	(0.017)	0.012	(0.018)	17496	7046	0.099
Cons. Plastics	0.003	(0.021)	0.000	(0.023)	13899	5879	0.080
Mineral Prods.	−0.016	(0.011)	−0.004	(0.014)	68894	24267	0.000
Ferr. Smelting	−0.015	(0.020)	−0.015	(0.017)	16489	6820	0.002
Nonferr. Smelt.	0.034*	(0.020)	0.020	(0.021)	11506	4639	0.070
Metal Prods.	0.035**	(0.018)	0.032*	(0.019)	34608	13729	0.110
Equipment	0.006	(0.015)	0.005	(0.016)	50828	19280	0.018
Spec. Equipment	−0.024	(0.020)	−0.012	(0.019)	25937	10042	0.005
Transport	−0.004	(0.015)	−0.009	(0.014)	33316	12060	0.003
Electric Eq.	0.025*	(0.014)	0.038**	(0.015)	42325	15438	0.152
Electronics	0.018	(0.015)	0.006	(0.015)	23339	8538	0.171
Instruments	0.019	(0.038)	0.009	(0.039)	9309	3414	0.124
Handicraft	0.009	(0.024)	0.035	(0.025)	13858	5457	0.022

Dependent variable is export/output. Firm fixed effect regressions. All regressions include year dummies and control for firm fixed effects, firm size (logged number of employees), firm age, and leverage (total debt as share of total asset). Robust standard errors in parentheses; $*p < 0.10$, $**p < 0.05$, $***p < 0.01$.

100% in the metal products industry, for example, will increase the ratio of export to total sales by just over 3 percentage points. This is a rather small effect given that the average share of foreign sales in the end of our sample period, 2006, is about 23% and that in some industries this share just exceeds 50% on average. Again, one potential explanation for the small effect of FDI shares on exports is the control of firm fixed effects, which may have captured part of the effect on exports.

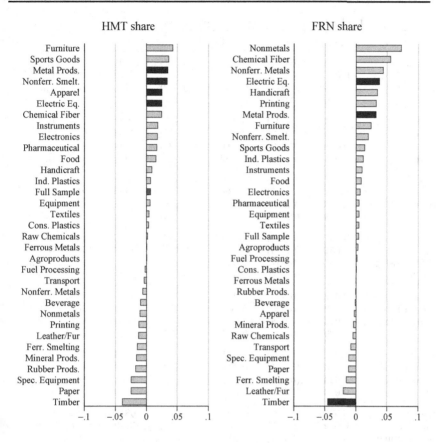

Figure 2.4 Effects of FDI on exports: Full sample.
Note: Dark bars represent coefficients that are statistically significant at least at 10% level.

The overall effect of FRN investment, on the other hand, is insignificant. This result is consistent with the story that foreign investment from other parts of the world into China is largely market access-driven FDI, where the main purpose of the investment is to facilitate entry to the large domestic market in China. Different FRN effects are found for different industries. Specifically, we find positive spillovers on exporting activity in target firms in metal products and electric equipment, while we find a negative significant effect for firms in timber industry. This negative effect may be driven by a limited amount of foreign investment in that industry.

Since the majority of the firms in our sample do not have any foreign share, the results are likely driven by the initial foreign investment into

Table 2.9 Effect of FDI on exports: Foreign firms.

Sector	HMT share		FRN share		N	N_g	r2_o
Full Sample	0.004	(0.007)	0.002	(0.007)	149691	52568	0.044
Nonferr. Metals	−0.041	(0.029)	0.004	(0.020)	72	37	0.008
Nonmetals	0.043	(0.054)	0.170**	(0.072)	281	113	0.000
Agroproducts	−0.000	(0.030)	0.003	(0.029)	6314	2140	0.001
Food	0.041	(0.027)	0.038	(0.027)	3922	1304	0.001
Beverage	−0.019	(0.022)	−0.013	(0.020)	2155	641	0.026
Textiles	0.004	(0.022)	0.004	(0.023)	13553	4843	0.017
Apparel	−0.044*	(0.026)	−0.080***	(0.026)	14938	5389	0.013
Leather/Fur	0.041	(0.039)	0.031	(0.039)	6875	2453	0.039
Timber	−0.022	(0.048)	−0.034	(0.047)	2460	915	0.001
Furniture	−0.035	(0.069)	−0.048	(0.066)	2561	931	0.012
Paper	−0.058	(0.040)	−0.044	(0.043)	3644	1203	0.005
Printing	0.037	(0.034)	0.080**	(0.037)	2148	649	0.113
Sports Goods	0.052	(0.064)	0.051	(0.065)	4367	1518	0.070
Fuel Processing	−0.034	(0.037)	−0.038	(0.039)	445	154	0.013
Raw Chemicals	−0.008	(0.024)	−0.013	(0.023)	8733	2920	0.011
Pharmaceutical	0.032	(0.025)	0.013	(0.024)	2885	938	0.005
Chemical Fiber	−0.062	(0.050)	0.008	(0.072)	664	261	0.004
Rubber Prods.	−0.072	(0.068)	−0.046	(0.068)	1624	574	0.020
Ind. Plastics	0.029	(0.032)	0.037	(0.032)	3791	1450	0.061
Cons. Plastics	−0.026	(0.033)	−0.024	(0.033)	4753	1847	0.040
Mineral Prods.	−0.013	(0.021)	0.008	(0.022)	7332	2461	0.018
Ferr. Smelting	−0.023	(0.044)	−0.031	(0.035)	1188	444	0.000
Nonferr. Smelt.	0.079*	(0.044)	0.065	(0.047)	1210	482	0.014
Metal Prods.	0.020	(0.039)	0.024	(0.037)	6859	2473	0.056
Equipment	0.059**	(0.027)	0.062**	(0.027)	7062	2567	0.023
Spec. Equipment	−0.027	(0.033)	−0.011	(0.032)	4207	1663	0.019
Transport	−0.017	(0.034)	−0.028	(0.034)	5612	1912	0.006
Electric Eq.	0.048**	(0.024)	0.058**	(0.024)	9356	3340	0.092
Electronics	0.003	(0.027)	−0.001	(0.027)	12057	4277	0.078
Instruments	0.049	(0.039)	0.037	(0.038)	3218	1085	0.185
Handicraft	−0.044	(0.042)	−0.021	(0.040)	4709	1701	0.009

Dependent variable is export/output. Firm fixed effect regressions. All regressions include year dummies and control for firm fixed effects, firm size (logged number of employees), firm age, and leverage (total debt as share of total assets). Robust standard errors in parentheses; $*p < 0.10$, $**p < 0.05$, $***p < 0.01$.

the target firms. To see whether the size of foreign investment matters, we now restrict the sample to firms that have nonzero HMT or FRN share. The results are reported in Table 2.9 and Figure 2.5. We still find that the effects of foreign investment are statistically significant only in a few

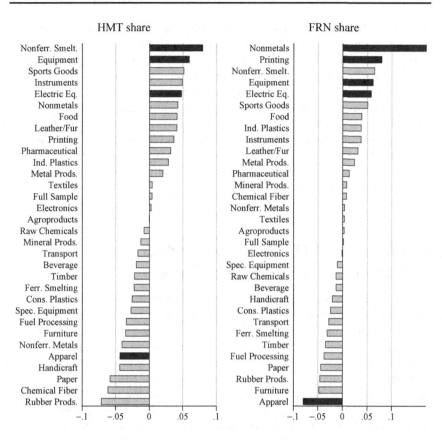

Figure 2.5   Effects of FDI on exports: Foreign firms.
Note: Dark bars represent coefficients that are statistically significant at least at 10%
level.

industries. Although the share of FRN now has a significant positive effect
in more industries than the share of HMT, neither type of FDI has an
overall significant effect on firms from all industries.

When specific industries are studied, we find that a higher share of
investment from HMT is associated with a higher share of exports in total
sales of firms in general equipment and electric equipment industries, while
it is associated with a lower share of exports in total sales of firms in
apparel. For firms producing apparel, we also find a negative effect of foreign
investment from FRN, but we find positive effects of FRN share on export
of firms in nonmetal mineral processing, printing, and general and electric
equipment.

We check the robustness of the results using other alternative specifications — for example, dropping leverage, replacing it with log(asset), etc. — and obtain very similar results. These results on exports thus help shed light on the goals of foreign investors into China — foreign investors from the Greater China Area tend to use the target firms as a stepping stone for exports, while for investors from outside the Greater China Area it is likely that FDI is market-seeking. Interestingly, for industries such as apparel it appears that firms with a small share of foreign investment are seeking an export platform. Firms with a larger share of foreign investment, on the other hand, appears to have a market-seeking motive, leading to a lower share of exports in target firms' sales.

2.4. Effects of FDI on New Product Introduction by Target Firms

In the last section of this chapter, we study an effect that has increasingly drawn attention from both academics and policy makers, namely, how FDI influences target firms' innovation behaviors. From the standpoint of the host country, especially developing economies such as China, foreign capital embodies more advanced technology. Thus, FDI may lead to more innovation. On the other hand, several arguments suggest that the opposite should be expected. First, foreign capital moving into a less developed country is usually attracted by its cheap labor, thus the technology brought in with the investment is most likely of the mature kind, involving less innovation. In addition, in the event that foreign investors would like to engage in innovation in the target firms, the frequently lax intellectual property protection in the host country will usually give them pause. These forces combine to reduce the incentive for innovation in foreign-invested firms.

We explore this issue empirically in this section, again using the NBS manufacturing census for 2000–2006, which provides information on the output of new products for all years except in 2004. Consistent with the analysis above, we estimate the effects of foreign investment from Hong Kong, Macao, or Taiwan separately from those of FDI from other foreign countries. And similarly, we estimate the effects separately for each industry, controlling for firm and year-fixed effects. The dependent variable is a dummy variable indicating whether the firm has positive new product sales in a certain year, and the additional controls include firm size (measured as log of number of employees), firm age, and leverage. In other specifications, we use the ratio of new product sales to total sales as the dependent variable and obtain very similar results. In the interest of space, we only

Table 2.10 Effects of FDI on new product introduction by target firms: Full sample.

Sector	HMT share		FRN share		N	N_g	r2_o
Full Sample	0.001	(0.003)	−0.002	(0.003)	745330	278081	0.031
Ferrous Metals	0.014	(0.009)	−0.001	(0.010)	4450	2056	0.007
Nonferr. Metals	−0.020	(0.019)	−0.078	(0.058)	4168	1766	0.018
Nonmetals	0.003	(0.030)	0.001	(0.050)	6539	2757	0.018
Agroproducts	−0.022*	(0.012)	−0.016	(0.013)	46693	18418	0.029
Food	−0.038*	(0.020)	−0.032	(0.020)	17387	6487	0.033
Beverage	0.005	(0.028)	0.010	(0.032)	13067	4699	0.049
Textiles	−0.000	(0.009)	0.001	(0.010)	67440	25027	0.025
Apparel	−0.004	(0.008)	−0.016**	(0.008)	37188	13631	0.016
Leather/Fur	0.007	(0.012)	0.010	(0.012)	18378	6894	0.012
Timber	−0.005	(0.019)	−0.012	(0.025)	14006	6066	0.017
Furniture	0.002	(0.017)	0.011	(0.021)	8292	3243	0.021
Paper	−0.024**	(0.012)	−0.021*	(0.012)	24610	8691	0.018
Printing	−0.013	(0.012)	0.003	(0.016)	16166	5678	0.022
Sports Goods	−0.002	(0.019)	−0.002	(0.020)	9992	3636	0.011
Fuel Processing	−0.036	(0.036)	0.012	(0.037)	5183	2079	0.017
Raw Chemicals	0.001	(0.014)	0.009	(0.016)	55669	20094	0.031
Pharmaceutical	0.033	(0.031)	0.014	(0.030)	17010	5654	0.084
Chemical Fiber	0.022	(0.073)	0.014	(0.065)	3200	1241	0.106
Rubber Prods.	0.043	(0.049)	0.026	(0.046)	8055	2945	0.010
Ind. Plastics	0.024	(0.018)	0.024	(0.021)	17597	7074	0.016
Cons. Plastics	−0.019	(0.016)	−0.008	(0.017)	14111	5915	0.018
Mineral Prods.	−0.007	(0.013)	0.011	(0.014)	69376	24387	0.030
Ferr. Smelting	0.046	(0.037)	−0.013	(0.059)	16610	6860	0.028
Nonferr. Smelt.	0.008	(0.023)	−0.035	(0.029)	11572	4660	0.023
Metal Prods.	0.024	(0.015)	0.022	(0.016)	35122	13815	0.017
Equipment	0.046**	(0.021)	0.031	(0.020)	51134	19335	0.069
Spec. Equipment	−0.011	(0.028)	−0.006	(0.030)	26095	10079	0.063
Transport	0.012	(0.022)	−0.006	(0.023)	33587	12105	0.076
Electric Eq.	−0.000	(0.014)	−0.012	(0.017)	42729	15504	0.045
Electronics	−0.007	(0.015)	−0.018	(0.016)	23759	8597	0.055
Instruments	0.069**	(0.033)	0.057*	(0.033)	9488	3431	0.039
Handicraft	0.003	(0.019)	0.000	(0.020)	14518	5553	0.014

Dependent variable is new product output/output dummy which is equal to one if new product output/output is positive and zero otherwise. All regressions include year dummies and control for firm fixed effects, firm size (logged number of employees), firm age, and leverage (total debt as share of total assets). Robust standard errors in parentheses; $^*p < 0.10$, $^{**}p < 0.05$, $^{***}p < 0.01$.

report coefficients on foreign shares. As usual, Chapter 8 gives details of the estimation procedures and variable definitions.

Table 2.10 and Figure 2.6 give results for the full sample of firms, which show no overall significant direct effects of foreign investment on new

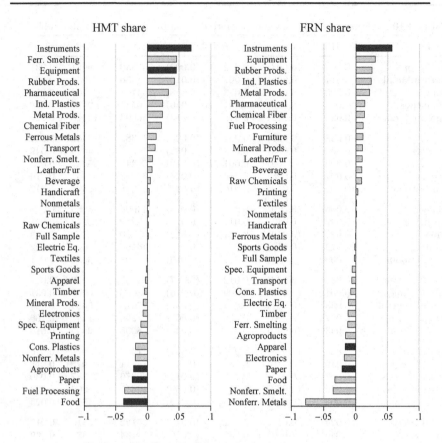

Figure 2.6 Effects of FDI on new product introduction by target firms: Full sample. *Note*: Dark bars represent coefficients that are statistically significant at least at 10% level.

product sales, either positive or negative. For target firms in specific sectors, there are significant effects, some positive and some negative. Compared to domestic firms, firms with foreign investment from both FRN and HMT regions are more likely to report new product sales in the instrument sector, while those in the paper industry are less likely to report new product sales. In addition, firms with HMT investment also tend to be less innovative in food and agroproducts, but more innovative in equipment, while firms with FRN investment tend to be less innovative in apparel.

We also limit our sample to firms with positive foreign shares and rerun the estimations, with results shown in Table 2.11 and Figure 2.7. Again, there is no overall significant effect on firm innovation for either

Table 2.11   Effects of FDI on new product introduction by target firms: Foreign firms.

Sector	HMT share		FRN share		N	N_g	r2_o
Full Sample	0.004	(0.007)	−0.000	(0.007)	153433	53057	0.022
Nonferr. Metals	0.000	(0.000)	0.000	(0.000)	76	38	
Nonmetals	−0.040	(0.062)	−0.087	(0.093)	284	113	0.010
Agroproducts	−0.052*	(0.027)	−0.041	(0.029)	6491	2162	0.004
Food	−0.030	(0.039)	−0.024	(0.037)	3998	1319	0.016
Beverage	−0.055	(0.041)	−0.066*	(0.039)	2166	643	0.064
Textiles	0.002	(0.019)	0.003	(0.019)	13843	4879	0.015
Apparel	0.011	(0.015)	−0.002	(0.014)	15675	5477	0.013
Leather/Fur	0.055**	(0.022)	0.060***	(0.023)	7214	2490	0.001
Timber	−0.056*	(0.032)	−0.050	(0.033)	2537	922	0.007
Furniture	−0.025	(0.056)	−0.018	(0.058)	2660	938	0.020
Paper	−0.023	(0.028)	−0.029	(0.030)	3681	1206	0.021
Printing	0.010	(0.026)	0.025	(0.028)	2160	651	0.013
Sports Goods	0.031	(0.026)	0.040	(0.027)	4604	1556	0.006
Fuel Processing	−0.110*	(0.061)	−0.032	(0.054)	447	154	0.007
Raw Chemicals	−0.025	(0.033)	−0.022	(0.033)	8802	2932	0.039
Pharmaceutical	0.059	(0.063)	0.051	(0.056)	2910	941	0.082
Chemical Fiber	−0.025	(0.144)	−0.003	(0.147)	664	261	0.000
Rubber Prods.	−0.031	(0.102)	−0.051	(0.108)	1672	578	0.001
Ind. Plastics	0.024	(0.036)	0.015	(0.035)	3840	1461	0.011
Cons. Plastics	−0.008	(0.043)	−0.003	(0.044)	4888	1866	0.005
Mineral Prods.	0.012	(0.029)	0.027	(0.030)	7434	2473	0.035
Ferr. Smelting	−0.083	(0.105)	−0.148	(0.132)	1191	446	0.095
Nonferr. Smelt.	0.068	(0.058)	0.033	(0.065)	1215	483	0.007
Metal Prods.	−0.046*	(0.026)	−0.051*	(0.027)	7048	2500	0.020
Equipment	0.053	(0.036)	0.045	(0.037)	7139	2580	0.066
Spec. Equipment	−0.003	(0.068)	0.016	(0.068)	4236	1668	0.057
Transport	−0.024	(0.046)	−0.046	(0.047)	5682	1923	0.083
Electric Eq.	0.053*	(0.031)	0.040	(0.033)	9537	3366	0.019
Electronics	0.015	(0.033)	0.002	(0.033)	12361	4317	0.026
Instruments	0.101	(0.071)	0.090	(0.072)	3305	1093	0.007
Handicraft	−0.008	(0.041)	−0.001	(0.040)	4951	1725	0.014

Dependent variable is new product output/output dummy which is equal to one if new product output/output is positive and zero otherwise. Sample is restricted to firms with positive HMT and/or FRN shares. All regressions include year dummies and control for firm fixed effects, firm size (logged number of employees), firm age, and leverage (total debt as share of total assets). Robust standard errors in parentheses; $^*p < 0.10$, $^{**}p < 0.05$, $^{***}p < 0.01$.

the HMT-invested firms or the FRN-invested firms, with positive effects observed for some industries and negative effects observed for other industries. These industries mostly do not overlap with the sectors where significant effects are found for the full sample, but the main message from

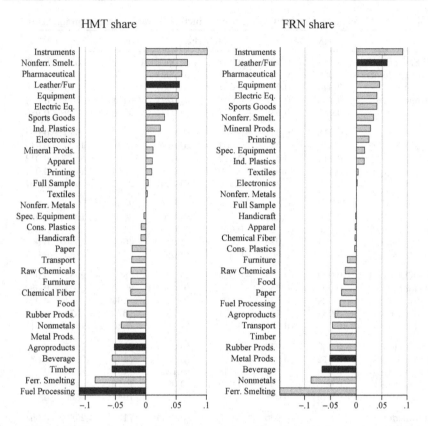

Figure 2.7 Effects of FDI on new product introduction by target firms: Foreign firms. *Note*: Dark bars represent coefficients that are statistically significant at least at 10% level.

the results is clear: On average, foreign-invested firms do not have a higher probability of developing new products. Furthermore, these results are robust when using other alternative specifications, for example, dropping leverage, replacing it with log(asset), and so on.

An important caveat of the above analysis is that we only have information on new product introduction by the firm. While the product may be new for the firm, it might not be new from the consumer's point of view — in fact, new product introduction may represent either true innovation or imitation of a product already made by another firm, such as the acquiring firm for example. In Chapter 6 we go into greater length to separate the effects on innovation and imitation by domestic firms, using a theoretical model and an alternative data set.

2.5. Summary

In this chapter we show that investment from Hong Kong, Macau, and Taiwan is as likely to increase as to decrease firms' TFP, while investment from outside Greater China Area tends to substantially increase productivity. We also find that foreign investment increases wages of target firms, but only for skilled workers. By paying higher wages, foreign-invested firms also manage to attract higher quality skilled labor. In addition, we show that for a few industries foreign investment has a positive impact on exporting activity, especially investment from HMT. However, the positive effects on exports are quite small in size. Finally, we show that on average foreign-invested firms are not more likely to develop new products, whether the investment is from HMT or other regions.

Some of the findings are in line with the literature, but others are quite novel. In particular, this is the first study to differentiate the FDI effects on skilled versus unskilled labor in foreign-invested firms, and it also provides the first piece of evidence for the lack of wage effects for production workers. Although positive effects are found for HMT investment, the small size of positive effects on exports is also quite surprising. Finally, this is the first systematic study that shows the absence of positive or negative effects of FDI on new product introduction in target firms.

Chapter 3

FDI Spillovers on Productivity of Domestic Firms

China has been the world leader among developing countries in attracting FDI over the past decade. During this period, the Chinese economy has boomed. In Chapter 2 we demonstrated that foreign capital inflows have increased productivity of target firms, especially when the foreign capital comes from outside of the Greater China Area. This leads to a related question: To what extent have the productivity benefits of these FDI flows spilled over to indigenous Chinese firms either in the same industry (horizontal externalities) or in upstream or downstream industries (vertical externalities)?

As discussed in Chapter 1, the research on technological spillovers from FDI shows weak and inconclusive results in general and for China in particular. In this chapter, we try to reconcile some of these results by making use of the best available data and the state-of-the-art methodology. More importantly, we will rely on disaggregated analysis that distinguishes among sources of FDI, ownership types of domestic firms, and the industries of operation. This approach allows us to see where exactly spillover effects of FDI on TFP can be found and what determines how they are distributed along the various dimensions.[1]

One major difficulty in previous studies stems from the use of aggregate level data, which often include both foreign and domestic firms, and thus cannot distinguish the higher productivity of foreign firms from the positive spillover effects on domestic firms. Even when the two groups of firms can be separated, one cannot reject the possibility that the observed positive effects are due to the initially more productive domestic firms in locations attracting more foreign capital. Such reverse causality or omitted variable bias is present if a cross-section of firm-level data are used, due to potential "cherry-picking" by foreign investors of locations that have higher productivity potential not observable to an econometrician. Moreover, if it takes

---

[1]This chapter is coauthored with Hirotaka Miura.

time for positive FDI spillovers to take effect, any cross-section analysis will miss them.

To better address these issues, we employ *firm-level panel* data from the Chinese NBS manufacturing census of medium-sized and large firms (2000–2006) described in detail in Chapter 8. Using firm-level panel is essential for multiple reasons. First, firm fixed effects can be controlled for, so that the effect of FDI presence is identified by within firm changes in productivity variables, thus addressing the possibility of reverse causality or selection, to the extent that foreigners' investment decisions are based on initial firm conditions that do not vary over time. Second, seven years of data allow for the study of dynamic effects, which is crucial as various kinds of FDI spillovers all need time to materialize. Importantly, to avoid contamination from the firms that actually received foreign capital, we exclude from our regression sample all firms that had a nonzero share of foreign capital in any year during our sample period.

The firm-level data also allow us to disaggregate our analysis in four dimensions, all of which help us better understand the specific mechanisms that determine FDI spillovers. First, domestic firms may be affected by FDI presence in sectors other than their own through supplier or client relations. Thus we do not limit our analysis to horizontal spillovers, but also analyze the effects of upstream and downstream presence of foreign firms, which we refer to as "vertical spillovers." We note that measures of horizontal and vertical FDI presence are highly correlated even though we exclude "own industry" when computing vertical measures. Therefore, for the ease of interpretation we estimate separate regressions for vertical and horizontal spillover effects.

Second, we analyze the effects of the presence of capital from the Greater China Area separately from those of capital from other foreign countries for two reasons: to account for the fact that some Greater China Area FDI may be round-tripping capital, and to acknowledge potentially different technological gaps between these two regions and mainland China. Third, we analyze separately domestic firms that are private and those that are state-owned, because it is likely that private firms will be more susceptible to technological spillovers. And fourth, we estimate spillover effects, both vertical and horizontal, for each two-digit China Industrial Code (CIC) industry separately and repeat our analysis for subsamples of private and state-owned firms in each industry. For pharmaceuticals, electronics, transportation equipment, and plastics, we further separate them into subgroups of three-digit CIC industries.[2] We drop industries such as coal, petroleum,

---

[2]See Chapter 8 for specific reasons why these industries are split into finer subgroups.

and tobacco due to large shares of state-controlled firms and the extremely small shares of foreign firms.

3.1. Estimation Specification and Measurement of FDI Presence

As discussed in Chapter 2, the state-of-the-art method for estimating total factor productivity is dynamic system GMM with firm fixed effects, which we also adopt in this section's analysis (see Chapter 8 for more technical details of the method). Based on the estimated TFP, we then regress it on the average measures of FDI presence, limiting our sample to domestic firms only. Specifically, we estimate the following regression for horizontal spillovers:

$$Y_{ispt} = \alpha_i + \alpha_t + \beta_1 AFRN_{spt-1} + \beta_2 AHMT_{spt-1} + \mathbf{Z}'_{ispt}\Gamma + \varepsilon_{it}, \qquad (3.1)$$

where Y is the TFP of firm i in sector s province p and year t; $AFRN$ is the measure of average presence of FDI from outside of the Greater China Area in sector s province p, and $AHMT$ is the corresponding measure for FDI from the Greater China Area, both lagged by one year; $\mathbf{Z}$ is a vector of control variables at the firm level; while the error term ε_{it} is allowed to be AR(1) (see Chapter 8 for more detailed discussion). Note that both firm and year fixed effects are controlled for in the estimation.

As stated above, we estimate these regressions for the full sample, and for private and SOE firms, separately. We also conduct the analysis by sector, again for all firms, and for private and SOE firms, separately. Coefficients β_1 and β_2 thus measure the effects of foreign presence on our outcome variables conditional on firm heterogeneity, common time effects, and control variables.

Another key element of the spillover analysis is the measurement of FDI presence. Following the literature, we first determine a range within which the effects of FDI presence are important, which we refer to as the "sphere of influence" for FDI spillovers. We then compute the average of foreign shares in the sphere of influence and use it to measure the FDI presence for domestic firms within the same sphere.

In studying horizontal spillovers, we focus on the same province and two-digit CIC industry cell as the sphere of FDI spillovers, and compute the average foreign share of all firms (weighted by output, asset, or employment) in the province-industry cell as our FDI presence measure. In other words, the horizontal spillover effects of foreign-invested firms on domestic firms located in the same province and two-digit CIC industry cell are the main target of our study. For example, we will limit to how the FDI presence in a given industry in a given province will impact that same province's domestic firms in the same industry. In doing this, we may miss broader spillover effects such as the effects of foreign-invested firms operating in other industries of the same province as well as the effects of foreign-invested firms in other provinces, be they in the same industry or not.

Our study of vertical FDI spillovers picks up part of the slack by looking at the effects of foreign-invested firms in the same province operating in other sectors, but we do not explore how foreign-invested firms outside of the province may affect domestic firms, be they in the same industry or not. In particular, we may miss the within-sector FDI spillovers caused by foreign-invested firms outside the province, although it is hard to say whether such an omission will lead to an underestimate or an overestimate of the total spillover effects. Because such within-sector effects could be dominated by competition or demonstration and learning, and because such effects may differ across industries, our specific way of defining the "sphere of influence" may have different implications on different industries.

Yet it is important to emphasize that our choice of "sphere of influence" is appropriate for achieving one of the main research goals in the current study. In particular, we want to highlight the importance of cross-industry differences in studying FDI effects in the host country. First of all, by focusing on province-two-digit CIC industry cells, we are able to compute FDI presence levels for these cells, which further allows us to estimate FDI spillovers for each two-digit CIC industry individually and to compare them with those for the whole economy. As we will show both in the current chapter and later chapters, different industries experience drastically different spillover effects, which will be infeasible to capture in a study based on industry-level FDI presence at the national level. Furthermore, certain patterns emerge from the industry-specific results that may guide future research. These findings suggest that certain industry characteristics may help explain the existence and direction of FDI spillovers. Although some of the future research questions may be better studied using a different definition for "sphere of influence" (such as national level FDI within the same industry), the current approach is crucial in producing the insights for future research decision-making.

3.2. Empirical Results

In this section we report the results of our parametric analysis. Since we estimate a large number of regressions — nine for each industry, which we present in Tables 3.1–3.3 — we will discuss the results based on the graphical representation of the estimated coefficients shown in Figures 3.1–3.3, as we have done in Chapter 2.

3.2.1. Horizontal spillovers

Horizontal spillover effects may arise due to competition and demonstration effects. When foreign capital flows into the industry, domestic firms might find more competition in both input and output markets. Competition in the output markets may lower measured TFP (by lowering output prices) but may also increase actual TFP by creating incentives for firms to increase efficiency. Competition in the input markets, such as the market for skilled labor, is likely to lower measured TFP through an increase in cost of inputs (see Hale and Long, forthcoming and Chapter 4 of this book). Demonstration effects are expected to be positive, as they describe ways in which domestic firms learn superior technologies and management practices from foreign-invested firms through observation, worker mobility, formal contracting, and informal interaction.

To estimate such horizontal FDI spillovers, the FDI measures are computed as the average foreign share for the same industry (in the same province). Our results for the regressions are presented in Table 3.1 and Figure 3.1. An important observation is that although the overall FDI spillover effect is small and nonsignificant, there are both positive and negative effects that are statistically significant — in some industries demonstration effects seem to dominate, while in others competition effects are more prevalent. On the other hand, private firms overall enjoy positive FDI spillovers, while no significant effects are observed for the overall sample of SOEs.

Looking more closely, we can see that there are slightly more positive spillovers and fewer negative spillovers from foreign investment from outside the Greater China Area (FRN) than from investment from Hong Kong, Macao, and Taiwan (HMT). For both FRN and HMT spillovers, we find small but statistically significant positive spillover effect in the subsample of private firms, consistent with the distribution of coefficients for private firms skewed more toward positive than for SOEs or for the full sample of domestic firms.

Focusing on specific industries, we find that spillovers from the FDI from both the Greater China Area and the rest of the world are positive and statistically significant for industrial plastics and electric equipment industries when we look at the full sample of domestic firms. And a few additional industries enjoy positive and significant spillovers from FRN but not from HMT, including furniture, sports goods, and mineral products.

Table 3.1 Horizontal spillovers from FDI on productivity.

Sector	L.HMT All dom.	L.FRN All dom.	Obser-vations All dom.	Firms All dom.	L.HMT Private	L.FRN Private	Obser-vations Private	Firms Private	L.HMT SOE	L.FRN SOE	Obser-vations SOE	Firms SOE
Full Sample	−0.008	0.023	569878	220674	0.069**	0.099***	239416	114162	−0.022	−0.131	58231	22773
Ferrous Metals	−0.393	1.040	4481	2077	−2.387	0.535	1755	1075	−1.931	3.312	380	129
Nonferr. Metals	−0.352	−0.039	4039	1714	−1.825***	0.561	927	524	−2.972**	−2.577***	705	304
Nonmetals	−0.627	−0.219	6377	2696	0.367	0.439	1760	998	−0.594	−0.057	1108	390
Agro-products	−0.043	−0.016	39181	15957	0.195	−0.028	14860	7416	−0.068	−0.009	6621	2813
Food	0.025	0.017	12706	4985	0.102	0.093	4221	2088	0.088	−0.022	2288	954
Beverage	0.082	0.081	10752	4025	0.462	0.120	3414	1631	−0.269	0.468	2127	864
Textiles	−0.333*	−0.165**	50067	19427	−0.272	0.006	27105	12272	1.237	0.699	2383	1049
Garments	0.097	−0.066	19397	7701	0.044	−0.006	9998	4719	0.897***	0.201	611	242
Leather/Fur	0.160	0.159	10224	4214	0.065	0.232	5874	2799	0.238	−1.396	250	111
Timber	−0.125*	0.009	11270	5116	−0.171	−0.004	5711	3018	0.159	−0.552*	689	310
Furniture	0.091	0.136*	5265	2211	−0.051	−0.019	2456	1264	0.030	0.399	269	103
Paper	0.110	0.070	20327	7393	0.058	0.109	8127	3690	0.213	0.357	1240	500
Printing	0.143	0.207	14593	5059	0.239	0.455	3862	1850	0.158	0.553	5104	1608
Sports Goods	−0.039	0.156*	4870	1971	−0.377*	−0.039	2590	1200	0.330	0.305	208	87
Fuel Processing	0.154	0.033	4672	1922	−0.035	−0.186	1639	863	−0.171	0.196	414	168
Raw Chemicals	0.072	0.173	45449	16889	0.029	0.112	17502	8255	−0.028	0.640*	4798	1911
Pharmaceutical	−0.137	−0.078	13427	4606	−0.073	0.201	3835	1773	−0.057	0.033	1776	763
Chinese Meds.	−0.305	−0.415***	5176	1899	−0.297	0.072	1393	668	−2.952*	0.701	719	343
Western Meds.	0.160	0.190	7026	2550	0.062	0.530	2023	976	0.912	0.018	942	419

(Continued)

Table 3.1 (*Continued*)

Sector	L.HMT All dom.	L.FRN All dom.	Obser-vations All dom.	Firms All dom.	L.HMT Private	L.FRN Private	Obser-vations Private	Firms Private	L.HMT SOE	L.FRN SOE	Obser-vations SOE	Firms SOE
Chemical Fiber	−0.025	−0.273**	2384	953	−0.121	0.108	1257	598	−0.557	0.187	174	83
Rubber Prods.	−0.034	0.028	6127	2326	0.020	−0.028	2534	1194	0.761*	0.774	440	173
Ind. Plastics Prods.	0.289**	0.176*	13186	5502	−0.015	0.106	6014	2941	0.870	−0.023	731	335
Cons. Plastics	−0.089	0.115	8730	3945	−0.236***	−0.029	4695	2412	−0.136	0.954	235	103
Mineral Prods.	0.160	0.196*	61028	21785	0.333	0.264	21933	10119	−0.007	0.080	6657	2546
Ferr. Smelting	−0.303	−0.382	15186	6358	−0.128	−0.117	6851	3509	−1.150*	−0.444	958	362
Nonferr. Smelt.	0.117	0.131	10194	4165	0.245	0.139	4287	2194	0.769	−0.607	655	271
Metal Prods.	−0.057	0.144	27155	11148	0.415***	0.390**	12422	6119	−0.773**	−1.332	1152	487
Equipment	−0.161	−0.063	43681	16749	0.307**	0.368***	20373	9468	−0.114	−0.708	4258	1567
Spec. Equipment	−0.003	−0.112	21645	8367	0.271	0.115	8614	4096	0.017	−0.577	3584	1299
Transport	−0.292**	−0.064	27505	10108	−0.024	0.041	10174	4714	−0.606*	−0.321	4211	1588
Autos	−0.222	0.032	15272	5992	−0.247	0.034	5839	2847	−0.407	−0.626	2017	823
Electric Eq.	0.130*	0.155*	30946	11626	0.139*	0.174**	13347	6192	−0.028	−0.167	1774	715
Electronics	−0.090	−0.035	10109	3997	0.260***	0.246***	4015	1954	−0.678**	−0.666***	1190	468
Telecom	0.065	0.068	1862	727	0.434	0.451	624	312	−1.339***	−0.719**	244	99
Computers	−0.061	0.097	844	394	−0.014	0.207	277	163	2.113***	1.415***	85	41
Instruments	−0.026	0.020	5931	2308	0.142	0.144	2476	1164	−0.064	−0.269	870	338
Handicraft	−0.061	0.163	8904	3673	−0.169	0.354	4676	2213	0.026	−0.239	368	158

Dependent variable is TFP. All regressions include year dummies and firm fixed effects. Standard errors are clustered on province and two-digit CIC sector codes.

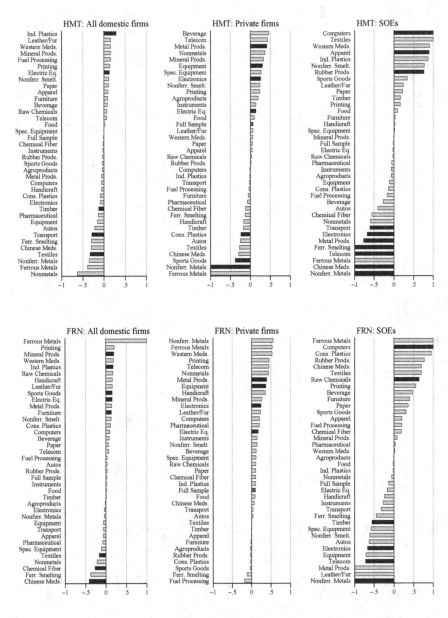

Figure 3.1 Horizontal spillovers from FDI on productivity.
Note: Dark bars represent coefficients that are statistically significant at least at 10%
level.

But for the textile industry, the FDI spillover effects are significantly negative, regardles of the origin of the foreign capital. For firms in Chinese medicine and chemical fiber, the spillover effects of FRN are negative and significant, but not those of HMT. Conversely, the spillover effects are negative and significant for timber and transportation industries for HMT, but not for FRN.

Now we look at results for the subsamples of private firms versus SOEs. For electronics, metal products, equipment, and electric equipment, we find positive and significant spillovers for private firms, but negative or insignificant spillovers for state-owned firms. For telecommunication equipment, timber, Chinese medicine, and transportation industries, SOEs have negative and significant spillovers, while private firms have no significant spillover effects. In the nonferrous metals industry, the spillovers from both FRN and HMT are negative and statistically significant for SOEs, but only significantly negative for HMT in private firms. On the other hand, for the computer, garments, and rubber products industries we find positive spillovers for SOEs only; and for sports goods and consumer plastics industries, we find negative spillovers for private firms only.

We will discuss the patterns behind these findings in the next section, together with the findings on vertical spillovers. It is worth pointing out, however, that many of the results on horizontal spillovers are as expected. First, we would expect that private firms are more flexible and stand to gain more from demonstration effects of FDI and to compete against foreign firms than state-owned firms. Thus, we would expect more positive horizontal spillovers for private firms and more negative horizontal spillovers for SOEs. We definitely see these differences on Figure 3.2 overall and in examples of metal products and electronic industries (including equipment, electric equipment, and electronics).

Second, we should expect more technological spillovers from FRN than HMT for two reasons. Theoretically, because the technological differences between the Greater China Area and mainland China are arguably not as large as between the rest of the world and the mainland China, the potential for learning is thus smaller with FDI from Hong Kong, Macao, and Taiwan, resulting in relatively more positive spillovers from FRN than HMT. In addition, FDI from the HMT region is more likely to be round-tripping FDI, implying little technological advantage over domestic firms. Empirically, results from Chapter 2 provide further evidence that firms with FDI from outside the Greater China Area are more likely to have higher total factor productivity, which is the source for technological learning by domestic firms that are close by. Again, we see some support for this in the results, especially for private firms, and in furniture, sporting goods, as well as mineral products industries for the whole sample.

Table 3.2 Vertical spillovers from FDI on productivity: Backward linkages.

Sector	L.HMT All dom.	L.FRN All dom.	Observations All dom.	Firms All dom.	L.HMT Private	L.FRN Private	Observations Private	Firms Private	L.HMT SOE	L.FRN SOE	Observations SOE	Firms SOE
Full sample	-0.038	0.026	569878	220674	0.116**	0.155***	239416	114162	-0.091	-0.337**	58231	22773
Ferrous metals	-0.628	-0.115	4481	2077	2.737	0.920	1755	1075	-2.166***	-6.603**	380	129
Nonferr. metals	-2.504**	-0.004	4039	1714	-2.964	2.648	927	524	-3.354	-2.390	705	304
Nonmetals	-0.967***	0.473	6377	2696	-0.809	1.088	1760	998	-2.555***	0.938	1108	390
Agro-products	0.366	-0.114	39181	15957	1.069*	-0.019	14860	7416	1.008	0.316	6621	2813
Food	0.328	0.122	12706	4985	0.194	-0.145	4221	2088	0.059	0.432	2288	954
Beverage	1.452**	1.088*	10752	4025	1.727	0.639	3414	1631	2.180	-0.480	2127	864
Textiles	-0.191	-0.034	50067	19427	0.022	0.219	27105	12272	1.187	1.267	2383	1049
Garments	-0.126	-0.038	19397	7701	0.366**	0.435**	9998	4719	1.917**	0.389	611	242
Leather/fur	0.035	-0.057	10224	4214	0.370	0.190	5874	2799	-0.775	-7.692***	250	111
Timber	-0.379**	-0.097	11270	5116	-0.335	0.066	5711	3018	2.768**	-0.243	689	310
Furniture	-0.078	0.006	5265	2211	-0.183	-0.232	2456	1264	0.508	-1.138	269	103
Paper	0.028	-0.087	20327	7393	0.003	-0.159	8127	3690	0.834	0.661	1240	500
Printing	-0.052	-0.055	14593	5059	0.132	0.015	3862	1850	0.296	-0.007	5104	1608
Sports goods	0.455*	0.548**	4870	1971	0.858**	1.056***	2590	1200	1.781*	1.770**	208	87
Fuel Processing	-0.206***	0.955	4672	1922	-0.385***	0.424	1639	863	-0.146	-2.065	414	168
Raw chemicals	0.118	0.143	45449	16889	0.336*	0.276	17502	8255	0.359	0.046	4798	1911
Pharmaceutical	0.451***	0.247*	13427	4606	0.737**	0.841**	3835	1773	0.283	-0.187	1776	763
Chinese meds.	0.294	-0.127	5176	1899	-0.012	0.710	1393	668	-0.015	0.518	719	343
Western meds.	0.466**	0.413*	7026	2550	1.351**	1.163***	2023	976	0.298	-0.123	942	419

(Continued)

Table 3.2 (*Continued*)

Sector	L.HMT All dom.	L.FRN All dom.	Obser-vations All dom.	Firms All dom.	L.HMT Private	L.FRN Private	Obser-vations Private	Firms Private	L.HMT SOE	L.FRN SOE	Obser-vations SOE	Firms SOE
Chemical fiber	-0.057	0.098	2384	953	0.728**	0.185	1257	598	-1.458	0.939	174	83
Rubber prods.	0.288	0.251	6127	2326	0.075	-0.056	2534	1194	-1.559	-1.617	440	173
Ind. plastics	0.063	0.021	13186	5502	-0.138	-0.073	6014	2941	-0.737	-0.985	731	335
Cons. plastics	-0.057	0.097	8730	3945	-0.272	-0.019	4695	2412	4.351*	4.401	235	103
Mineral prods.	0.060	0.148	61028	21785	0.148	0.231	21933	10119	-0.309	-0.353	6657	2546
Ferr. smelting	-0.432*	-0.053	15186	6358	-0.005	0.443**	6851	3509	-0.094	-1.539**	958	362
Nonferr. smelt.	0.044	0.207	10194	4165	0.274	0.362	4287	2194	-0.195	-0.988	655	271
Metal prods.	0.028	0.093	27155	11148	0.123	0.247**	12422	6119	-0.984	-0.777	1152	487
Equipment	-0.173*	0.009	43681	16749	0.109	0.188**	20373	9468	-0.479	-0.734*	4258	1567
Spec. equip-ment	0.024	-0.157	21645	8367	0.376*	0.173	8614	4096	-0.172	-1.172**	3584	1299
Transport	-0.120	0.005	27505	10108	0.133	0.160	10174	4714	-0.283	-0.063	4211	1588
Autos	-0.091	0.089	15272	5992	-0.048	0.177	5839	2847	-0.067	-0.301	2017	823
Electric eq.	0.167	0.155	30946	11626	0.103	0.135	13347	6192	0.490*	0.325	1774	715
Electronics	-0.060	-0.001	10109	3997	0.253***	0.235***	4015	1954	-0.753***	-0.691**	1190	468
Telecom	-0.038	-0.013	1862	727	0.356	0.364	624	312	-1.329***	-0.630*	244	99
Computers	-0.025	0.132	844	394	-0.159	0.072	277	163	2.281***	1.490***	85	41
Instruments	-0.098	-0.053	5931	2308	0.162	0.113	2476	1164	-0.442	-0.091	870	338
Handicraft	0.247	0.478	8904	3673	0.428	0.593	4676	2213	4.493**	6.008	368	158

Dependent variable is TFP. All regressions include year dummies and firm fixed effects. Standard errors are clustered on province and two-digit CIC sector codes.

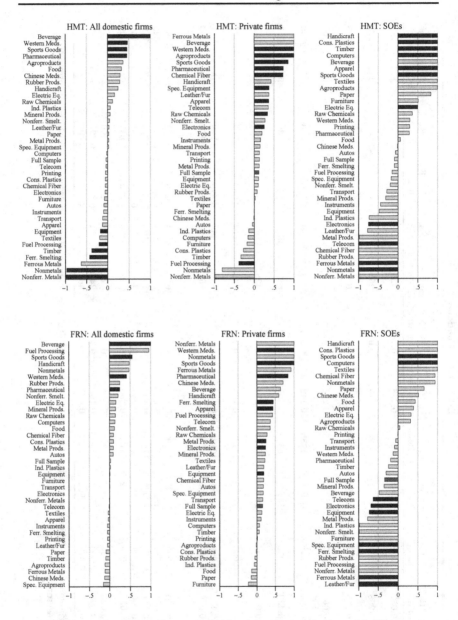

Figure 3.2   FDI spillovers on productivity through backward linkages.
Note: Dark bars represent coefficients that are statistically significant at least at 10%
level.

3.2.2. Backward linkages

Spillovers through backward linkages occur because the demand for the output of upstream domestic firms is likely to increase in response to foreign entry in the downstream industries, raising production volume and thus productivity if there are economies of scale. Moreover, foreign firms may help upstream firms improve their technology in order to produce inputs and parts to their specifications. In some cases, foreign firms even provide their suppliers with technological blueprints: According to a survey of Chinese firms conducted by the World Bank in 2001, over 25% of Chinese domestic firms that produced parts or other inputs for foreign firms, used licensed technologies or processes provided by foreign firms to introduce new process improvements.[3] There may be some negative impact as well, however, if foreign firms demand higher quality inputs, which may lower domestic firms' productivity if it takes them time to adjust or if some of their output are rejected. Competition effects are unlikely in the case of backward linkages, because domestic firms and foreign-invested firms are in sufficiently different industries and therefore do not compete directly on input or output markets.

To measure the presence of FDI in downstream industries, we construct for each industry i the weighted average foreign share of all industries that use industry i's output. The weights for the downstream industries are the corresponding complete output coefficients from the Input–Output table for China, and the FDI measures thus constructed are referred to as the downstream FDI presence, or the backward linkage FDI measures. The estimation methods and specifications are otherwise similar to those used for studying horizontal spillovers (see Chapter 8 for more detailed discussion).

Our results for the regressions where FDI measures are for the downstream industries are presented in Table 3.2 and Figure 3.2. We can see that, compared to horizontal spillovers, there are more positive than negative effects and that most of the positive effects are concentrated in private firms. On average, we find positive and statistically significant spillover effects through backward linkages in private firms for FDI from both regions, while we find negative and statistically significant effects of downstream FRN presence for state-owned firms. We believe this could be due to the fact that SOEs are on average older and less flexible and therefore stand

---

[3]*Source*: Author's computations based on the survey data from the Study of Competitiveness, Technology, and Firm Linkages, World Bank (2001).

to gain less from foreign presence downstream. Moreover, foreign firms may prefer to deal with private firms than with SOEs and therefore spillovers through backward linkages to SOEs will be limited. Finally, as we include FDI measures that are lagged only one period, it may be the case that it takes SOEs longer to adjust and to begin benefitting from foreign presence downstream. But in the meantime, they have to shoulder the adjustment costs to serve foreign firms, while at the same time competing with domestic firms in the same industry whose productivity has benefited from the downstream FDI presence. These forces may thus combine to result in the negative downstream FDI spillovers.[4]

More specifically, we find positive and statistically significant spillovers from downstream presence of foreign capital from both regions for beverage, sporting goods, and pharmaceuticals (western medicine, but not Chinese medicine), as well as for private firms in garment industry and state-owned firms in the computer industry. And just like for horizontal spillovers, we find positive spillovers from downstream FDI for private firms but negative spillovers for SOEs in electronics. We also find negative backward linkages for SOEs in ferrous metals and telecom industries, regardless of the origin of the foreign capital. Findings in industries including nonmetal products, garments, leather and fur, chemical fiber, ferrous smelting, metal products, equipment, and special equipment are also consistent with the general finding of more positive spillovers (or fewer negative spillovers) in private firms than in SOEs. On the other hand, more positive spillovers (or fewer negative spillovers) are found in SOEs than in private firms in the following industries: timber, fuel processing, consumer plastics, electric equipment, and handicraft. Overall, we see more positive backward FDI linkages for private firms than for SOEs.

3.2.3. Forward linkages

The most obvious reason for spillovers through forward linkages is the availability of higher quality inputs. In addition, more sophisticated inputs may be associated with higher TFP because they may allow for superior technologies to be applied in the production process. Negative spillover effects may arise because some adjustment may be required to incorporate new inputs into production processes, which can be costly in the short run.

To estimate the spillover effects of upstream FDI presence, we construct the FDI measure as the average foreign shares of all industries that supply the industry of our interest based on the Input–Output table for China,

---

[4]Unfortunately, due to a relative short time span of our data we cannot fully investigate the possibility of SOEs benefitting from downstream FDI presence in a longer time period.

which is referred to as the upstream FDI presence or the forward FDI linkage. The estimation method and specifications are again similar to those used in the previous sections. As usual, see Chapter 8 for the more detailed description.

Our results for the regressions where FDI measures are for the upstream industries are presented in Table 3.3 and Figure 3.3. The patterns we find are similar overall to those for backward FDI linkages — there are more positive spillovers and they are widespread for private firms, but not for the SOEs. Just like for backward linkages, we find on average positive and statistically significant spillover effects through forward linkages for private firms for FDI from both regions, while we find negative and statistically significant effects of upstream FRN presence for state-owned firms. Once again, we believe that SOEs may have less interaction with foreign suppliers, and even if they do, they may be less flexible and may take longer to adjust to new types of inputs. In the meantime, the higher productivity of private firms in the same sector implies greater competition and thus negatively impacts the SOEs' productivity.

In addition, we find a small but statistically significant positive effect of FRN for the full sample of domestic firms. Industries enjoying positive forward linkages for FRN but not for HMT capital include fuel processing, rubber products, nonferrous smelting, and handicraft, while industries suffering negative forward linkages for HMT but not for FRN capital are nonferrous metals, nonmetal products, timber, and consumer plastics. The opposite pattern of positive forward linkage for HMT but not FRN capital is observed only in Chinese medicine. As before, the larger positive spillovers from FRN are likely reflecting greater technological advantage of capital from outside the Greater China Area.

We find positive spillovers from upstream presence of FDI from both regions in beverage, sporting goods, and electric equipment industries for the whole sample for firms. We also find positive FDI forward linkages for state-owned firms in computer and handicraft industries. For pharmaceuticals, we find positive spillovers that are driven only by western medicine in the case of FRN and by both western and Chinese medicine for HMT. As before, for electronics, we find positive spillovers for private and negative spillovers for state-owned firms, as well as negative spillovers for state-owned firms producing telecommunication equipment. As with backward linkages, we find positive effects from both HMT and FRN presence upstream for private firms and negative effects from FRN presence upstream for state-owned companies producing specialized equipment.

Overall, we observe more positive forward FDI linkages for private firms and for foreign capital from outside the Greater China Area. But for SOEs, the forward FDI linkages for foreign capital from outside the

Table 3.3 Vertical spillovers from FDI on productivity: Forward linkages.

Sector	L.HMT All dom.	L.FRN All dom.	Obser-vations All dom.	Firms All dom.	L.HMT Private	L.FRN Private	Obser-vations Private	Firms Private	L.HMT SOE	L.FRN SOE	Obser-vations SOE	Firms SOE
Full sample	0.020	0.070**	569878	220674	0.128***	0.154***	239416	114162	−0.078	−0.271**	58231	22773
Ferrous metals	−0.124	−0.072	4481	2077	0.309	−0.132	1755	1075	−0.932	−1.278	380	129
Nonferr. metals	−0.403*	0.057	4039	1714	−0.039	0.709	927	524	−0.577	−0.078	705	304
Nonmetals	−1.203**	0.424	6377	2696	0.289	0.456	1760	998	−1.228	0.667	1108	390
Agro-products	1.163	0.100	39181	15957	1.670*	0.025	14860	7416	5.479	1.889	6621	2813
Food	0.700	0.427	12706	4985	0.545	0.038	4221	2088	0.145	−1.549	2288	954
Beverage	1.978*	1.670*	10752	4025	3.617**	2.136	3414	1631	2.986	−0.413	2127	864
Textiles	−0.176	−0.070	50067	19427	−0.199	−0.015	27105	12272	0.822	0.785	2383	1049
Garments	0.001	0.007	19397	7701	1.223	1.338	9998	4719	5.370*	3.817	611	242
Leather/fur	−0.087	−0.197	10224	4214	0.563	0.292	5874	2799	−2.239	−12.932*	250	111
Timber	−0.439*	−0.138	11270	5116	−0.351	0.084	5711	3018	2.541	−1.742	689	310
Furniture	−0.031	0.115	5265	2211	−0.093	−0.142	2456	1264	0.828	−0.234	269	103
Paper	0.073	0.017	20327	7393	−0.020	−0.114	8127	3690	0.915	0.816	1240	500
Printing	−0.005	−0.019	14593	5059	0.200	0.093	3862	1850	0.351	−0.002	5104	1608
Sports goods	0.438**	0.502**	4870	1971	0.843***	1.004***	2590	1200	0.436	0.394	208	87
Fuel processing	0.339	0.684**	4672	1922	−0.098	0.363	1639	863	1.562	0.442	414	168
Raw chemicals	0.065	0.093	45449	16889	0.174	0.164	17502	8255	0.218	0.046	4798	1911
Pharmaceutical	0.379***	0.212**	13427	4606	0.563***	0.560***	3835	1773	0.216	−0.061	1776	763
Chinese meds.	0.383**	0.042	5176	1899	0.321	0.504	1393	668	−0.146	0.098	719	343
Western meds.	0.336*	0.269*	7026	2550	0.670*	0.558*	2023	976	0.551	0.254	942	419

(Continued)

Table 3.3 (*Continued*)

Sector	L.HMT All dom.	L.FRN All dom.	Firms All dom.	Observations All dom.	L.HMT Private	L.FRN Private	Observations Private	Firms Private	L.HMT SOE	L.FRN SOE	Observations SOE	Firms SOE
Chemical fiber	−0.066	0.007	953	2384	0.400*	0.116	1257	598	−1.048	0.541	174	83
Rubber prods.	0.158	0.166*	2326	6127	0.143	0.061	2534	1194	−0.408	−0.334	440	173
Ind. plastics	0.012	−0.013	5502	13186	−0.163	−0.106	6014	2941	−0.305	−0.678	731	335
Cons. plastics	−0.238*	−0.084	3945	8730	−0.297**	−0.134	4695	2412	1.635	1.766	235	103
Mineral prods.	0.025	0.140	21785	61028	0.202	0.262	21933	10119	−0.750	−0.634	6657	2546
Ferr. smelting	−0.107	−0.005	6358	15186	0.121	0.214**	6851	3509	0.265	0.018	958	362
Nonferr. smelt.	0.106	0.169**	4165	10194	0.189	0.225	4287	2194	0.028	−0.293	655	271
Metal prods.	0.066	0.095	11148	27155	0.235	0.318*	12422	6119	−0.176	−0.029	1152	487
Equipment	−0.198	0.003	16749	43681	0.212	0.293**	20373	9468	−0.713	−0.978	4258	1567
Spec. equipment	−0.012	−0.220	8367	21645	0.534*	0.271	8614	4096	−0.275	−1.513**	3584	1299
Transport	−0.182	0.012	10108	27505	0.168	0.227	10174	4714	−0.769	−0.349	4211	1588
Autos	−0.094	0.157	5992	15272	−0.060	0.249	5839	2847	0.020	−0.592	2017	823
Electric eq.	0.203*	0.185*	11626	30946	0.147	0.141	13347	6192	0.388	0.196	1774	715
Electronics	−0.087	−0.028	3997	10109	0.274***	0.253***	4015	1954	−0.745***	−0.710**	1190	468
Telecom	−0.013	0.005	727	1862	0.421	0.428	624	312	−1.410***	−0.708*	244	99
Computers	−0.147	0.028	394	844	−0.101	0.129	277	163	2.272***	1.532***	85	41
Instruments	−0.114	−0.005	2308	5931	0.440	0.368	2476	1164	−0.975	−0.090	870	338
Handicraft	0.733	1.075**	3673	8904	0.693	1.089	4676	2213	9.322***	11.484*	368	158

Dependent variable is TFP. All regressions include year dummies and firm fixed effects. Standard errors are clustered on province and two-digit CIC sector codes.

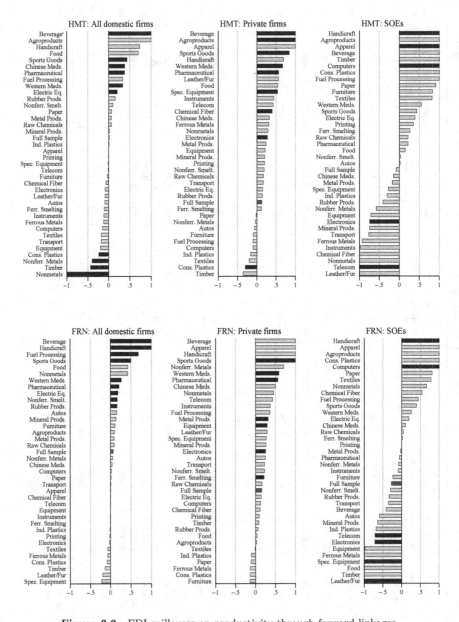

Figure 3.3 FDI spillovers on productivity through forward linkages.
Note: Dark bars represent coefficients that are statistically significant at least at 10% level.

Greater China Area are significantly negative, which is largely driven by the negative effects in leather and fur and special equipment industries.

3.3. Conclusion

While in the full sample spillover effects are small and rarely statistically significant, we do find positive spillovers from FDI in China on the productivity of domestic firms. However, such spillovers are distributed very unevenly across industries, types of spillovers (horizontal versus vertical), origins of foreign capital, and ownership structures of the domestic firms. More positive effects are observed for private firms; more vertical spillovers through backwards and forwards linkages are found than horizontal spillovers; and these spillovers tend to be larger when foreign capital comes from outside of the Greater China Area. When conducting the analysis across industries, we find evidence of both positive and negative horizontal spillovers.

The advantage of private firms in benefitting from positive spillovers is due to private firms' greater competitiveness. Larger effect of foreign capital from outside the Greater China Area is likely due to the bigger technology gap. On the other hand, negative effect of direct competition in the same industry explains the observed pattern with more positive results for vertical spillovers than for horizontal spillovers.

Less obvious are differences in results across industries. Specifically, we find that more technologically sophisticated industries, such as pharmaceuticals, experience on average more vertical spillovers, but not more positive horizontal spillovers, possibly because foreign firms in such industries are likely to guard their know-how more carefully. Positive horizontal spillovers are more likely to be obtained in industries that export more, potentially because of the reduced effect of competition in the domestic market. Vertical spillovers are also larger in industries with more exports, possibly because quality improvement that can arise from such spillovers are more important for export markets than for domestic ones. Moreover, the findings suggest that industrial structure, such as ownership composition of firms in the industry and the concentration ratio may also affect the extent of technological spillovers from FDI.

The fact that spillover effects are unevenly distributed across industries, ownership types, and sources of FDI helps us understand why there is such diversity of findings in the vast literature on FDI spillovers in China. The results using pooled or aggregate data depend on the sample of firms included in the study, the sample period, as well as the additional controls and restrictions used. We believe our analysis provides good reasons for further studies at the disaggregated level and we hope that it would encourage future empirical work in this direction.

Chapter 4

FDI Spillovers on Labor Markets

Along with spectacular GDP growth, China has experienced rapid increase in wages. Despite rising inequality, wages have increased even in the poorest provinces (Candelaria, Daly, and Hale, 2009). Thus it is natural to ask the question: How much of this increase in wages can be attributed to inflows of foreign capital? In Chapter 2, we showed that foreign-invested firms pay higher wages to their employees and tend to hire higher quality labor. In this chapter, we study how wages and labor quality composition of *domestic* firms are affected by the presence of foreign-invested firms in the same industry and geographical area.[1]

While most of the literature concentrates on the positive effects of FDI presence, the competition effects of FDI should not be overlooked. Aitken and Harrison (1999), for example, document competition effects in the output market in Venezuela: by competing away market share from domestic firms, foreign firms are believed to impose negative effects on indigenous firms in the host country, which may offset the positive technological spillovers transferred from foreign firms to domestic firms. In this chapter, we focus instead on the competition effects in the input markets. In particular, foreign firms may compete for labor inputs with indigenous firms on the domestic labor market and drive up the wage bill.

As shown in Figure 4.1, both real FDI capital utilization and real average wage in China have exhibited an upward trend in the last decade. Of course, the patterns shown in the figure could be due to a multiplicity of development areas that have simultaneously occurred in China during the same time period. A more rigorous study showing the competition effects of FDI on domestic labor market requires more disaggregated data. To date, there has been little direct evidence substantiating such competition effects on labor markets.

---

[1]Parts of the text in this chapter appeared in Hale and Long (forthcoming).

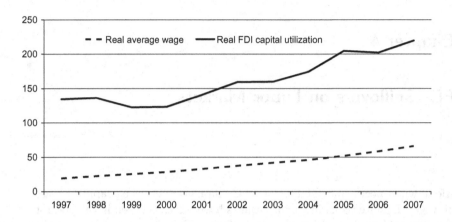

Figure 4.1   FDI capital utilization and average wages in China.
Source: Statistical Yearbook, various issues (Chinese National Bureau of Statistics).

Just as there has been mixed evidence about the *direct* effect of FDI on wages, i.e., tests of whether foreign-invested firms pay higher wages (see Chapter 2, Section 2.2), the analysis of *indirect* effects of FDI on wages in *domestic* firms also has failed to produce conclusive findings. Furthermore, to our knowledge there have been no studies of FDI effect on the quality of labor in domestic firms.

In this section, we attempt to fill in the gaps by studying the indirect effects of FDI presence on labor market outcomes in China, and by further analyzing the differential pressures that FDI puts on wages of different types of labor and the quality composition of labor. For such an analysis, we need variables in addition to the balance sheet information provided in the NBS manufacturing census. Thus, we make use of the *Study of Competitiveness, Technology and Firm Linkages* conducted by the World Bank in 2001, which includes comprehensive information on both wage and labor quality as well as firm performance. Chapter 8 gives more details of the World Bank survey.

Studies related to the analysis in this chapter include the following: Aitken, Harrison, and Lipsey (1996) examine U.S., Mexican, and Venezuelan firms and find no evidence of wage spillovers, while Blonigen and Slaughter (2001) also find no increase in demand for skilled labor due to inward FDI into the United States. On the other hand, Feenstra and Hanson (1997) study Mexican regions and find positive spillovers of FDI on skilled wages, while Barry, Görg, and Strobl (2005) observe differential effects on exporting and nonexporting firms among large Irish firms.

4.1. Firm Ownership and Personnel Practices in China

There are two aspects of Chinese labor market that we need to take into account when analyzing the data and interpreting the results. First of all, a firm's ownership type has important effects on employee salaries in China, because personnel practices in state-owned enterprises (SOEs) in China are likely to differ dramatically from those in private firms.

Kato and Long (2006) show that top executives are paid more in private firms than in SOEs, suggesting greater salary dispersion in domestic private firms than in SOEs. Indeed, as recently as 1999, the highest ratio between CEO compensation and that of an average production worker was six among the 40 largest enterprises owned by the central government.[2] In contrast, compensation data for private-listed firms in China and worker compensation data from the International Labor Organization suggest that the ratio was close to 15 between 1998 and 2002 for Chinese private firms.[3]

There are at least two potential explanations for such differences: (1) SOEs face constraints in their wage structures, i.e., they are not able to pay their skilled employees more due to constraints imposed through government policies and guidelines; and, (2) SOEs have multiple social objectives and thus are not willing to structure their wage scales at the cost of egalitarianism.

Both explanations given above are legacies of the planned economy. Before economic reforms began in the late 1970s, employee compensation in China followed a rigid grid system based on factors that reflected neither firm performance nor individual contributions, such as the region, industry, level of supervising government agency, and the size of the enterprise, as well as the job title, occupation, and seniority of the individual.

Even in the postreform era, compensation mechanisms in SOEs oftentimes are still subject to government guidelines that restrict wage differentials among employees and that often set a limit on the maximum salary for executives. For example, both the central government and several provincial governments in China have set or have considered setting limits on the ratio between CEO salary and production worker compensation. The limit being contemplated by the central government as of 2005 was 15, while

---

[2]See the "Research report on Chinese manager incentive mechanisms and policies," cited in the January 14, 2002, issue of the *Market Daily* (accessed online on July 26, 2006 at http://news.xinhuanet.com/newscenter/2002-01/24/content_252489.htm).

[3]We are not aware of any data on the ratio between CEO salary and production worker compensation for either SOEs or private Chinese firms in general.

provinces such as Jiangxi had adopted 10 as the ratio limit in the same year.[4]

As a comparison, almost a decade earlier the 1996–1997 Tower Perrin Compensation Survey gives the range of CEO–worker compensation ratio of 11 for Germany and 24 for the United States. To the extent that these numbers reflect the efficient outcomes of labor market competition in those countries and given the fact that China most likely is in greater need for managerial talents, these limits set by the government may impose artificial restrictions on SOEs' ability to hire and retain talents.

Although schemes to circumvent salary caps abound, big salaries for top executives are generally frowned upon by both the government and other employees in the state-owned firms. While private firms strive to increase firm value and thus base employee pay on individual productivity, state-owned firms have multiple social objectives to achieve, some of which (such as social stability) are more congruent with more equal pay schemes. In contrast, private firms in China have always enjoyed more freedom in setting their own compensation policies and have shown greater flexibility in adopting more effective incentive systems. (For further details on executive salary policies in Chinese firms, see Kato and Long, 2006.)

Whether it is the inability or the unwillingness on the part of the SOEs, the discussion above suggests that in reality private firms in China tend to have a more dispersed and more flexible wage distribution. And whether the more rigid and compressed wage structure in Chinese SOEs is due to explicit restrictions or implicit limitations, they have similar implications on how these firms compete on the labor market. When faced with firms that are both willing and able to pay higher wages for workers of higher quality, SOEs may experience difficulty in attracting and retaining quality employees.

The other aspect of the Chinese labor market worth exploring is the difference between unskilled labor and skilled labor. Although China has a rich endowment of *unskilled* labor, the shortage of *skilled* labor has been well documented. For example, according to the *Report on Chinese Entrepreneurs* issued by the Survey System for Chinese Entrepreneurs in 2003, 80% of the entrepreneurs surveyed report a shortage of technical personnel, over 50% report a shortage of managerial personnel, and 74% report a shortage of sales personnel. Therefore, a careful study of how FDI presence affects the

---

[4]See the March 25, 2005, Issue of *China Industry and Commerce Times*, and "The Rules for Administrating CEO Compensation in SOEs in Jiangxi Province," government document issued by the Jiangxi State Asset Supervision and Administration Commission (accessed online on July 21, 2006 at http://jiangxi.jxnews.com.cn/system/2006/07/07/002290697.shtml).

labor market in China should distinguish the two types of labor: unskilled and skilled.

To account for the variations in these two aspects, we study effects on wages and quality of skilled and unskilled labor separately. We also allow for FDI presence to have different effects on wages and quality of labor in domestic SOEs and private firms. We now explore the empirical validity of these implications.

4.2. Empirical Evidence

In this section we will show our findings with respect to the effects of FDI on labor market competition in China. We first present some information comparing the three groups of firms in China: SOEs, domestic private firms, and foreign-invested firms. Then we provide empirical findings on FDI spillovers in the labor market.

Table 4.1 shows the summary statistics of the variables from the World Bank firm survey data used in the analysis. Domestic firms with private ownership of less than 20% are listed as SOEs, while others are listed as private. This split corresponds most closely to the ownership types reported by the firms. This split is only done for the purpose of comparing the

Table 4.1   Labor characteristics by firm ownership.

Variable	Mean (SOE)	Mean (private)	Diff.	Foreign
	Domestic			
Log of Wage (prod. worker)	2.07	2.01	0.06	2.37
Log of Wage (engineer)	2.52	2.70	−0.18**	3.09
Log of Wage (manager)	2.54	2.68	−0.14*	3.16
Age (prod. worker)	34.6	30.5	4.0***	29.1
Age (engineer)	37.5	34.2	3.4***	32.8
Age (manager)	39.2	35.9	3.3***	35.1
Education (prod. worker)	9.84	9.56	0.28**	9.78
Education (engineer)	13.1	13.5	−0.32***	13.6
Education (manager)	12.6	12.7	−0.19*	13.1
Engineers with foreign experience	0.004	0.11	−0.006**	0.020
Managers with foreign experience	0.030	0.064	−0.034***	0.15
Skill ratio	0.31	0.36	−0.056***	0.35
Wage spread	0.44	0.58	−0.14**	0.66
Firm age	23.7	9.92	13.8***	8.30
Log of capital stock	9.63	8.21	1.42***	10.0
Log of labor force	5.60	4.76	0.84***	5.4
Observations[a]	326	792		382

Note: SOE is defined as private share <1, private $= not$(SOE).
*Significant at 10%; **significant at 5%; ***significant at 1%.
[a]Due to missing values, the number of observations for each variable may be smaller.

variables' summary statistics for domestic firms with different ownership in Table 4.1, while in the regression analysis that follows, we use a continuous measure of the share of private ownership.

The table shows that SOEs are quite different from private firms in many aspects: They tend to be larger and have a longer history; their employees tend to be older, and tend to get lower wages; and their managers tend to have less foreign work experience. These differences are all statistically significant. On the other hand, compared to domestic private firms, foreign firms hire even younger employees and pay even higher wages for all three groups (production workers, engineers, and managers). And the average education of engineers and managers and the percentage of them with foreign work experience are higher in foreign-invested firms. Finally, consistent with the previous discussion, the wage spread (measured as log(manager wage/production worker wage) is the largest in foreign-invested firms, followed by domestic private firms, and is the lowest in SOEs.

Before we discuss spillover effects of FDI presence on wages and quality of labor in domestic firms, we document more carefully the differences in these variables for domestic firms with respect to their ownership structure, by controlling for various firm and employee characteristics in a set of OLS regressions (see Chapter 8 for the detailed estimation specifications). Table 4.2 demonstrates that private firms tend to hire skilled labor of higher quality and pay them higher wages. Specifically, if the share of private ownership is higher, wages paid to engineers and managers, but not to production workers, are higher. We also find that employees of all types tend to be younger, the share of engineers and managers with foreign experience larger, and the managers more educated, while production workers tend to be less educated, if the private share is higher.

To discuss the magnitude of the above differences, we can compare firms with zero private share with those that have 100% private ownership share. The coefficients in the regressions reported in Table 4.2 indicate that wages of engineers are higher in private firms than in SOEs by about 17%, while the wages of managers are higher in private firms by about 20%. Note that some wage differences are due to differences in quality — when controlling for age, education, and foreign experience, the coefficients on private share in wage regressions for engineers and managers become smaller, with private firms paying wage by 12% and 15% higher for engineers and managers, respectively, than SOEs. The remaining average differences reflect the fact that age, education, and foreign experience only measure some of the quality aspects, with many others not observed by the researcher. In addition, private firms hire engineers and managers that are on average 2 and 4 years younger, respectively, after we control for firm age. The differences

Table 4.2 Labor differences between domestic private firms and SOEs.

Dependent variable	β(private share)	Robust S.e.	Controls	Adj.R^2	N.(obs)
Wage					
Log (avg. wage)					
Production workers	0.012	(0.093)	log(K/L)	0.07	793
Engineers	0.17**	(0.080)	log(K/L)	0.13	828
Managers	0.18***	(0.070)	log(K/L)	0.14	1076
Production workers	0.022	(0.10)	log(K/L), quality[a]	0.07	778
Engineers	0.10	(0.081)	log(K/L), quality[a]	0.13	790
Managers	0.13*	(0.074)	log(K/L), quality[a]	0.15	1013
Labor quality					
Average age					
Production workers	−5.00***	(0.59)	log(K), firm age	0.38	784
Engineers	−2.33***	(0.61)	log(K), firm age	0.27	830
Managers	−3.90***	(0.48)	log(K), firm age	0.27	1075
Avg. education					
Production workers	−0.28**	(0.13)	log(K)	0.21	789
Engineers	0.042	(0.12)	log(K)	0.18	831
Managers	0.29**	(0.11)	log(K)	0.25	1077
Avg. foreign experience					
Engineers	0.012**	(0.005)	log(K)	0.18	820
Managers	0.073***	(0.013)	log(K)	0.11	1050

*Significant at 10%; **significant at 5%; ***significant at 1%.
[a]Quality controls include average age, average age squared, and average education of the relevant group as well as controls for foreign experience for engineers and managers.
Estimated by OLS. City*sector-fixed effects included in all regression.
Sample limited to domestically owned firms.

in education level are modest: private firms hire managers that on average have four additional months of education, compared to SOEs, where average education of managers is 12.6 years. The average share of engineers and managers with foreign experience are 1 and 7 percentage points higher, respectively, in private firms than in SOEs.

We now turn to the spillover effects of foreign firm presence on domestic firms. The detailed description of the estimation method and specification is given in Chapter 8, but essentially we regress the average wage for a certain group of workers (skilled or unskilled) on the FDI presence measure, various firm characteristics, as well as labor quality controls. In particular, we include the interaction term of FDI presence and the firm's private share to allow for differential spillovers of FDI on firms of different ownership structures. Because of the cross-sectional nature of the data, we cannot control for firm fixed effects. We do, however, control for industry*region fixed effects. The FDI presence measure is also constructed at the industry*region level.

Table 4.3 presents the results from the analysis. The columns give coefficient estimates for private share, FDI presence, and the interaction term between private share and FDI presence. The rest of the columns report the included control variable list, the adjusted R^2, and the number of observations in each sample.

The top panel of Table 4.3 shows that private firms pay higher wages to both engineers and managers where there is more FDI, whereas SOEs only increase wages to engineers but not to managers. In contrast, FDI presence has no effect on the average wages of production workers in either private firms or SOEs.

The bottom panel of Table 4.3 summarizes the effects of FDI on average labor quality. For unskilled labor such as production workers, FDI presence has no significant effects on either their average age or their average education. In contrast, the presence of FDI tends to increase the education level of managers as well as their probability of having foreign work experience for private firms. The effects on the education level of engineers and managers in SOEs tend to be negative, whereas the effects on the average ages of these two groups tend to be positive, although the effects are not quite significant.

Combined together, these results suggest that the FDI presence has very different effects on the two types of labor markets in China — skilled versus unskilled — and very different effects on the two types of Chinese domestic firms — SOEs versus private firms. While there is evidence that the presence of FDI drives up the wages of engineers and managers (at least for some domestic firms), it does not have a significant effect on either the wages or the quality composition of production workers hired.

On the other hand, while private Chinese firms raise wages for their managers and engineers (potentially to compete with foreign-invested firms), SOEs do not seem to respond to the wage competition among managers or engineers imposed by foreign firms. Perhaps as a result of the different responses between private firms and SOEs, the average education level of managers hired by private firms and their probability of having prior foreign work experience are higher when there is FDI presence, whereas the same indicators for managers and engineers take up lower values for SOEs at the presence of FDI.

To understand the magnitudes of these effects, we compare the effects of an increase in FDI presence from 0% to 20% in the city–industry cell on fully private and fully state-owned firms. In private firms, such an increase

Table 4.3 Effect of FDI on labor of domestic private firms and SOEs (OLS).

	Coefficient on					
Dependent variable	Private shr.	FDI	FDI*Prv. shr.	Controls	Adj.R^2	N.(obs)
Wage						
Log (average wage)						
Production Workers	−0.079	0.60	0.20	log(K/L)	0.06	793
Engineers	0.057	1.17*	0.69	log(K/L)	0.11	828
Managers	−0.016	0.46	1.35**	log(K/L)	0.12	1076
Production Workers	−0.075	0.58	0.25	log(K/L), Quality[a]	0.06	778
Engineers	0.008	1.33*	0.50	log(K/L), quality[a]	0.11	790
Managers	−0.11	0.47	1.76***	log(K), quality[a]	0.13	1013
Labor quality						
Avg. Age						
Production Workers	−4.89***	3.31	−3.62	log(K), firm age	0.38	784
Engineers	−2.62**	3.22	0.56	log(K), firm age	0.27	830
Managers	−3.21***	1.40	−7.96	log(K), firm age	0.27	1075
Avg. Education						
Production Workers	−0.47*	−0.023	0.56	log(K)	0.20	789
Engineers	−0.066	−0.324	0.83	log(K)	0.17	831
Managers	0.046	−0.896	1.95*	log(K)	0.24	1077
Avg. Foreign Experience						
Engineers	0.003	−0.027	0.036	log(K)	0.001	820
Managers	0.049**	−0.001	0.30**	log(K)	0.08	1050

*Significant at 10%; **significant at 5%; ***significant at 1%. S.e. are clustered on city*sector cells.
[a]Quality controls include average age, average age squared, and average education of the relevant group as well as controls for foreign experience for engineers and managers. Estimated by OLS. City-fixed effects and sector-fixed effects included in all regression. Sample limited to domestically-owned firms.

in FDI presence would lead to 40–45% increase in wages of engineers and managers. For education, the average engineer in a typical private firm will have two more months of schooling, while the average manager will have five more months or schooling. In terms of foreign work experience, the manager's probability will increase by 6 percentage points for a typical private firm.

In contrast, for an SOE, the same increase in FDI increase will only lead to a 26% increase in engineer wages and only 10% increase in manager wages (which are not statistically significant). It would also lower average education of engineers and managers in SOEs by about one month and two months, respectively, and increase the average age of engineers and managers in SOEs by seven months or four months, respectively.

4.3. Robustness Tests and Discussion

The main concern with the data is that the measure of FDI presence is constructed using a small sample of firms. Thus, we are concerned that one large firm with or without foreign presence will substantially affect the average foreign share calculated for the city–industry cell. We therefore construct the alternative measure, for five manufacturing sectors only, using the census of manufacturing firms. We are comforted to find that the new measure is very similar to our original one: for the manufacturing sectors the simple correlation coefficient between the two FDI measures is 0.54, the adjusted R^2 of the regression of one measure on the other and city- and industry-fixed effects is 0.84, and the Spearman rank correlation coefficient is 0.64.

Since the new measure seems to be substantially higher than our original one for three sectors in Guangzhou and one sector in Tianjin, to test whether our results are sensitive to the differences in the FDI measure, we replace our original measure with the new measure for manufacturing sectors, while keeping the original measure for the service sectors. We are unable to estimate the model for manufacturing sectors only, because a small number of degrees of freedom is left when the sample is cut by half. All our results on labor quality hold both qualitatively and quantitatively. For the wage results, the p-values tend to increase because the new measure of FDI presence has higher variance, while qualitatively our results hold. We recover the statistical significance of the results if we instead use $\log(1 + \text{new measure})$ as the FDI indicator, which better matches the mean and the variance of our original measure.

In addition, we attempt alternative definitions of FDI presence using our original data set. First, we using the same measure of FDI presence as in the main specification, but for 2000 rather than for 1999. Our results are unchanged. Alternatively, we weigh the FDI share in each firm by the number of years since the firm first acquired a foreign partner, thus giving higher weight to FDI that was around for longer. We find that such modification does not affect our results much. We are thus fairly comfortable with the results reported in our main specification.

We also re-estimate wage regressions controlling for the hiring conditions of the firms, specific to each type of labor, such as minimum age, education, and experience of new hires, as well as the number of job applications per vacancy. While this restricts our sample, we find that our results are robust to including such controls.

Finally, because Barry, Görg, and Strobl (2005) show that FDI may have differential effects on wages of exporting and nonexporting firms, we re-estimate our regressions controlling for the share of foreign sales of each firm. We find that our results are not affected by the inclusion of this additional control variable.

4.4. Discussion of Empirical Findings

Our empirical findings give an affirmative answer to the following question — "Did Foreign Direct Investment Put an Upward Pressure on Wages in China?" While this particular result is quite straightforward, we also find some subtle and interesting patterns in the way FDI affects China's labor markets. In particular, we find that the upward pressure of FDI on wages is limited to the market for skilled labor, and that while private firms experience competition from foreign-invested firms as evidenced by higher wages of skilled workers, SOEs respond to such competition by hiring skilled workers of lower quality. In this section, we discuss our interpretations of these patterns.

Our finding that foreign firms pay higher average wages to skilled labor are consistent with the view that better technology used by foreign firms is complementary to skill and makes skilled labor more productive. In particular, we find the results to be more pronounced for managers than for engineers. This is consistent with the belief that foreign firms have superior managerial practices and therefore their managers in particular are more productive. Another potential reason for this finding is that foreign firms seek more productive managers and that age, education, and foreign experience do not fully account for differences in managers' productivity. In the latter case, more talented managers would be hired away from domestic firms and we would observe a decline in quality of managers in domestic firms where FDI presence increases, while the aggregate wage level need not increase. As the results in Table 4.3 demonstrate, there is evidence for such an effect. Therefore, FDI is likely to lead both to an increase in productivity as well as to competition with domestic firms in hiring skilled labor, thus a rise in the average wages of skilled labor, especially managers.

The findings with respect to the effect of private ownership share on wages and quality of labor in domestic firms are consistent with our discussion of hiring practices in China. In particular, we find that production workers are paid roughly the same in both types of firms, while engineers and managers are paid more in private firms, indicating relatively more compressed wage structure in SOEs. As we discussed, this could be due to either implicit or explicit wage constraints faced by SOEs in competing with other types of firms or to the inferiority of their skill-complementary factors of production. The finding that SOEs tend to employ lower quality skilled labor compared to private firms indicates that the wage compression in SOEs is more likely due to the implicit or explicit constraints on wages they can pay.

Furthermore, the average quality of managers for private firms tends to be higher where FDI is present. Since there is no robust evidence for deteriorating quality of managers in SOEs, these results seem to suggest that the supply of managers is more elastic than that for engineers. In particular, the inflow of FDI may have helped expand the pool of managers, especially those with foreign work experience. It is interesting that only private domestic firms benefit from the larger pool of managerial talent, but not SOEs. Our explanation for the difference is again the wage restrictions faced by SOEs.

In light of the above discussion of reasons for wage compression in SOEs and the cited reports on skilled labor shortages in China, we believe our results can be summarized as follows. Consider the impact of foreign firm entry on the labor market in the context of China, where SOEs face explicit or implicit constraints on wages or have inferior technologies that render skilled labor less productive. One potential effect of the FDI inflow is an increased demand for skilled labor. Since foreign firms are likely to use more skill-intensive technology and "greenfield" FDI increases demand for all factors of production, larger foreign presence in the city would lead to a higher demand for skilled labor. Given that in the short and medium run the supply of skilled labor is very inelastic, this would push the wages of skilled workers up in the city and industry with higher FDI presence. While private firms may raise wages of their skilled workers in order to retain them, SOEs might find it difficult because of explicit or implicit wage constraints. As a result, quality of skilled workers in SOEs would decline.

Of course, this is not the only story that is potentially consistent with our findings. For example, if foreign firms bring superior skill-complementary technology and that superior technology is adopted by domestic private firms but not by SOEs, we would observe similar patterns. In fact, the findings in Chapter 3 suggest that domestic private firms in China do benefit more from FDI spillovers in total factor productivity than SOEs, consistent with more technological transfer from FDI for private firms.

Two facts suggest that the constraints faced by SOEs in employment practices and their resultant disadvantage in competing with other firms on the labor market still play an important role in explaining our findings. First of all, we observe a decline in the quality of skilled labor in SOEs when more FDI is present, which is hard to explain by the differential in technological transfer from FDI alone. In addition, the inability of SOEs to hire and retain qualified employees is more likely one of the causes for their lower ability to benefit from positive FDI spillovers on productivity, rather than one of its consequences. In other words, labor mobility is one of the main mechanisms through which domestic firms learn from foreign firms and enjoy positive FDI spillovers, and the SOEs are less likely to benefit from such a mechanism due to the constraints in hiring and wage setting.

Overall, our results suggest that skilled labor is scarce and unskilled labor is abundant in China (at least at the time the survey was conducted). As a result, higher competition for skilled labor induced by foreign direct investment leads to higher wages of skilled labor both in foreign-invested and in domestic private firms that compete with foreign-invested firms for skilled labor. SOEs appear to be unable or unwilling to increase the wages they pay to their skilled workers and as a result experience a decline in the quality of their skilled personnel.

4.5. Conclusion

To summarize, we found that the FDI presence in China is putting an upward pressure on wages of skilled workers through increased competition in the market for skilled labor. Such competition effects are reflected in an increase in wages that private firms pay to their skilled workers and in a decline in quality of skilled labor in SOEs that appear to be constrained in terms of wages they can pay to their employees. We find no such competition effects in the market for unskilled production workers.

These findings suggest that labor market institutions such as wage constraints have important implications for how FDI affects domestic firms. To the extent that many developing countries have rigid labor market conditions, our findings help explain why it is particularly difficult to find positive FDI spillovers in these countries.

As an example, these findings offer one reason for why it is more difficult to find positive productivity spillovers from FDI for Chinese SOEs (see Chapter 3). If FDI leads to a lower quality of skilled workers in SOEs, these firms may lack the human capital necessary for absorbing potential technological spillovers. This in turn implies that quicker privatization may be necessary in order to capture potential positive spillovers from FDI.

Moreover, our findings may have important implications for income distribution in China. In particular, because FDI presence increases wages of better paid skilled workers, but does not have any significant positive effect on wages of production workers, more FDI presence is likely to lead to higher income inequality. This is, in fact, consistent with recent trends of an increasing skill premia and a growing rural–urban income inequality, because unskilled labor in China is largely drawn from the pool of rural population.

Chapter 5

FDI Spillovers on Exports of Domestic Firms

If China's fast economic growth in the past three decades has caught the attention of the world, then the rate of its export growth can only be described as breathtaking. Figure 5.1 illustrates growth of export from China in real terms since 2000, as compared with its GDP growth. It seems a conventional belief that China's economic growth in the last two decades was largely driven by a growing export sector. In this chapter we study how much of this growth can be attributed to foreign capital inflows. While in Chapter 2 we found that target firms of FDI in only a few industries have increased their exports in response to foreign investment, there is still a possibility that foreign presence in the same industry and province has had a more important effect on exporting activity of domestic firms.

Much like with other spillover effects, there are reasons for both positive and negative spillovers from the presence of foreign firms. Positive productivity spillovers may make domestic firms more efficient, which will allow them to explore business opportunities abroad. In addition to productivity improvement, learning in other aspects may also help domestic firms' increase exports. Swenson (2008), for example, argues that the presence of multinational firms may directly enhance the export capabilities of domestic firms by making it easier to learn about overseas markets and establish new connections. Chen and Swenson (2009) also show that proximity to multinationals tends to increase the unit value, which proxies for the quality, of new export transactions by domestic private firms.

On the other hand, the greater competition in both output and input markets brought by FDI presence may lead to negative effects on domestic firms' productivity and thus hamper their ability to sell overseas (Aitken and Harrison, 1999). In particular, foreign-invested firms compete with domestic firms in the global market, potentially even more vigorously than they do in domestic markets, which may result in negative effects of the FDI presence on the share of exports in total sales by domestic firms. In addition, some domestic exporters may switch to supplying foreign-invested

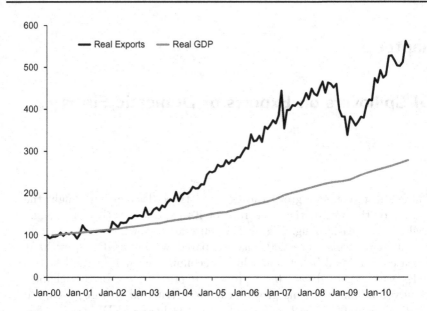

Figure 5.1   Dynamics of real GDP and real exports of China.
Source: Real exports data from the World Bank, Global Economic Monitor. Exports
Merchandise, Customs basis. Real GDP data from the Federal Reserve Board.

firms close-by to avoid additional costs involved in selling abroad. Thus we
will resort to the empirical analysis to study the spillover effects of FDI
presence on exports of domestic firms.

5.1. Empirical Results

To analyze FDI spillovers on exporting activities of domestic firms, we
will use the NBS manufacturing census data set for 2000–2006, which is
described in detail in Chapter 8. We adopt the same estimation method as
in Chapter 3 with one exception — because we do not have to estimate the
production function, we will use the linear regression model with firm fixed
effects, again as described in detail in Chapter 8. To allow for differential
effects along the various dimensions, in addition to estimations based on the
whole sample of firms, we will also analyze horizontal and vertical spillovers
by industry, by ownership type of domestic firms, and by source of foreign
investment (that from Greater China Area, HMT, or beyond, FRN). In
all regressions, our dependent variable is the share of exports in the firm's
total sales. In addition to firm fixed effects, we also control for the size
of the firm (number of employees), leverage (the ratio between total debt

and total asset), and age of the firm. In other specifications, we also drop leverage, or replace it with log of asset, and obtain very similar results. In order to control for common trends in time, we include year-fixed effects in the estimation. The construction of various measures for FDI presence is the same as in previous chapters, which is summarized in Chapter 8.

5.1.1. Horizontal spillovers

We begin our analysis in this chapter by looking at the effects of the presence of foreign-invested firms in the same industry and province, i.e., the horizontal spillover effects. Since exporting activity requires certain know-how that foreign firms can bring with them and because foreign firms are more likely to export than domestic firms (see Chapter 2, Section 2.3), the presence of such firms in the same industry and in the same location may benefit domestic firms that are trying to export their outputs. There is also the possibility of logistical synergies such as sharing containers or negotiating with the same intermediary. On the other hand, there may be a negative effect. Since, at least in some industries, foreign investment tends to increase exports and productivity, domestic firms in the same industry and location may be pushed out from the export market. Only data analysis can show which of these effects dominates.

Table 5.1 and Figure 5.2 present the results for horizontal spillovers, by industry, by ownership type, and by source of FDI. For FDI from the Greater China Area, we have mixed results for horizontal spillovers — positive for some industries and negative for others, while for FDI from the rest of the world, the spillovers are predominantly negative with two exceptions: private firms in apparel industry and state-owned firms in ferrous smelting, which tend to increase their share of foreign sales in response to an increase in FRN presence. The overall effect is negative for FRN — the spillover effect for the full sample is negative and significant.

For specific industries, positive spillovers from HMT on export activity are observed for the full sample and for private firms in textiles and furniture and for state-owned firms in pharmaceutical industry, especially those producing western medicine, as opposed to traditional medicine. These are the industries in which we did not find a significant effect of foreign investment on exports of target firms (see Chapter 2, Section 2.3), suggesting that the competition effect on the exporting market is unlikely to be present and therefore the positive spillover effect is likely to dominate. We observe negative spillovers of HMT on the export share of private firms in timber, mineral products, electric equipment, electronics industries, negative spillovers of HMT for state-owned firms in paper products, and negative spillovers of HMT for all firms in special equipment. In these industries,

Table 5.1 Horizontal spillovers from FDI on exports.

Sector	L.HMT All dom.	L.FRN All dom.	Observations All dom.	Firms All dom.	L.HMT Private	L.FRN Private	Observations Private	Firms Private	L.HMT SOE	L.FRN SOE	Observations SOE	Firms SOE
Full Sample	−0.014	−0.041***	593892	230656	−0.030	−0.044**	249177	118902	−0.009	−0.017	59231	23647
Ferrous Metals	0.028	−0.011	4644	2132	0.036	0.008	1817	1104	0.010	−0.100	392	131
Nonferr. Metals	−0.131	−0.231	4208	1785	−0.604	−0.926	976	549	0.017	0.102	735	316
Nonmetals	0.171	0.212	6531	2736	−0.226	0.143	1814	1022	0.029	0.043	1066	379
Agro-products	−0.021	−0.075	40646	16596	−0.007	−0.124**	15342	7680	−0.056	0.070	6742	2901
Food	−0.023	−0.049	13173	5236	−0.071	−0.073	4362	2177	0.026	0.082	2329	979
Beverage	0.058	0.026	10910	4164	0.106	0.022	3451	1659	−0.015	−0.063	2110	895
Textiles	0.280**	0.067	53646	20747	0.397*	0.074	28636	12933	0.104	0.152	2872	1234
Apparel	0.138	0.068	19849	8152	0.286	0.377**	10183	4938	−0.292	−0.081	592	248
Leather/Fur	−0.005	−0.088	10493	4431	−0.137	−0.311**	5988	2887	−0.088	−0.408**	258	118
Timber	−0.053	0.029	11701	5307	−0.261*	0.043	5903	3113	0.017	−0.011	703	324
Furniture	0.236*	0.044	5511	2340	0.330**	0.081	2544	1314	−0.089	−0.272	280	111
Paper	−0.037	−0.074*	21180	7681	−0.047	−0.169**	8475	3842	−0.364***	0.030	1271	515
Printing	−0.015	−0.038	14312	5157	−0.064	−0.130**	3989	1912	−0.024	−0.105	4588	1585
Sports Goods	−0.022	−0.195	4970	2087	−0.099	−0.161	2618	1247	−0.257	0.137	195	84
Fuel Processing	−0.001	0.045	4890	1994	0.004	0.009	1698	902	0.040	−0.018	426	172
Raw Chemicals	−0.025	−0.070	47520	17653	−0.075	−0.157*	18320	8631	0.048	0.057	4916	1974
Pharmaceutical	0.049	−0.034	14059	4908	0.100	−0.144	4027	1878	0.200*	0.080	1831	801
Chinese Meds.	0.051	−0.005	5449	2039	0.154	0.014	1465	715	0.261	−0.027	758	368
Western Meds.	0.076	−0.010	7328	2703	0.147	−0.265	2128	1026	0.208*	0.103	962	433

(Continued)

Table 5.1 (*Continued*)

Sector	L.HMT All dom.	L.FRN All dom.	Observations All dom.	Firms All dom.	L.HMT Private	L.FRN Private	Observations Private	Firms Private	L.HMT SOE	L.FRN SOE	Observations SOE	Firms SOE
Chemical Fiber	0.028	0.021	2541	1010	0.070	0.082	1328	632	−0.035	−0.063	201	91
Rubber Prods.	−0.027	−0.065	6395	2423	−0.082	−0.083	2631	1238	−0.012	0.053	447	181
Ind. Plastics	−0.017	−0.066**	13881	5759	0.008	−0.016	6269	3058	0.081	−0.131	780	355
Cons. Plastics	0.219	0.082	9130	4127	0.196	0.079	4872	2518	−0.085	−0.018	251	112
Mineral Prods.	−0.073	−0.106	63378	22596	−0.148**	−0.092	22816	10487	−0.182	−0.249	6766	2603
Ferr. Smelting	0.073	0.162**	15806	6594	0.016	0.055	7124	3630	0.327	0.436*	957	372
Nonferr. Smelt.	0.059	−0.035	10598	4305	0.152	−0.071	4469	2265	0.092	0.164	639	270
Metal Prods.	0.032	−0.198**	28166	11578	−0.025	−0.042	12819	6319	0.022	−0.171	1200	515
Equipment	−0.102	−0.061	44890	17269	−0.066	0.037	21128	9798	−0.004	0.042	4164	1588
Spec. Equipment	−0.017	−0.120***	22222	8629	−0.171**	−0.123**	8909	4229	−0.105***	−0.058	3615	1316
Transport	−0.024	−0.001	28303	10463	−0.098	−0.026	10543	4876	0.045	−0.033	4221	1630
Autos	−0.063	−0.014	15840	6219	−0.057	−0.046	6041	2952	−0.206	−0.044	2053	853
Electric Eq.	−0.113***	−0.114***	33322	12470	−0.183***	−0.161***	14143	6570	−0.044	−0.046	2072	841
Electronics	−0.011	−0.016	10798	4316	−0.097***	−0.089**	4223	2057	−0.041	−0.062	1253	496
Telecom	0.005	0.017	1926	771	0.040	0.101	652	329	0.080	0.079	222	97
Computers	−0.057	−0.171	913	428	−0.157	−0.218	303	178	0.585	0.217	90	44
Instruments	−0.151*	−0.156**	6167	2409	−0.206	−0.194	2573	1217	0.109	−0.038	935	357
Handicraft	0.138	−0.206	9061	3818	0.272	−0.180	4753	2288	0.303	0.049	378	162

Dependent variable is export/output. All regressions include year dummies and control for firm fixed effects. RHS also includes log of number of employees, total debt as share of total assets, and firm age in years. Coefficients are not displayed for presentation purposes. Standard errors clustered on province and two-digit CIC sector code in parentheses; $^*p < 0.10$, $^{**}p < 0.05$, $^{***}p < 0.01$. Private firms defined as firms with majority individual share. State-owned enterprises (SOEs) defined as firms with majority state share.

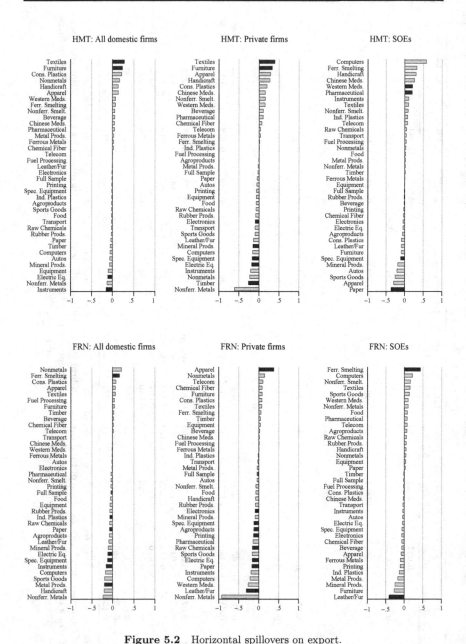

Figure 5.2 Horizontal spillovers on export.

Note: Dark bars represent coefficients that are statistically significant at least at 10% level.

it appears that competition effect dominates. In fact, with the exception of timber, these are the sectors where we found in Chapter 2 that FDI from the Greater China Area tends to increase exports of target firms, thus potentially making it more difficult for domestic firms to compete on export markets.

Negative effects of FRN presence are all concentrated in the private sector, with one exception of SOEs in leather and fur industry. This may not be surprising — state-owned firms are less likely to be subjected to foreign competition on export markets because their exports are facilitated by state-owned trading companies and because these firms are likely to have well-established trading partnerships. Private firms' exports, however, seem to be harmed by the presence of firms from outside of the Greater China Area. These negative effects are statistically significant for firms in agroproducts, leather and fur, paper products, printing, raw chemicals, special and electric equipment, and electronics. A positive coefficient on apparel is not surprising — this is the industry with relatively low capital and technological requirements in which small private firms can compete.

Our findings appear to be in sharp contrast with those of Swenson (2008) and there are a number of possible reasons for why the results from the two studies are different. On the technical side, the data sources and sample periods are different in the two studies: Swenson (2008) focuses on 1997–2003 time period, while our sample covers 2000–2006; she uses product-level customs data on exports, while we use firm balance sheet data. More importantly, however, she is asking a different question and her findings are, in fact, rather subtle. Specifically, she finds that domestic private firms are more likely to explore new export destinations or to develop new products for export when they have more contact with foreign-invested exporters.

While she interprets these findings as supporting evidence for the positive impact of FDI presence on domestic firms' export performance through information spillovers, the findings from her study are also consistent with an alternative explanation, which leads to a less sanguine conclusion on foreign firms' role in affecting domestic firms' exports. As Swenson does not look at the total value of exports by domestic firms, it is just as likely that domestic firms have shifted to new export products or destinations, precisely because they have been negatively impacted in the existing export markets due to increased competition brought by foreign-invested firms. Thus without looking at the overall effects on total exports of domestic firms, it is impossible to evaluate whether FDI presence plays a positive or negative role in promoting total export performance of domestic firms.

Similar and even more nuanced results are found by Mayneris and Poncet (2010), who also point out that spillovers are absent from the processing trade and are only present in ordinary trade activity — another reason why our data, in which we are not able to separate processing from ordinary trade, produce different results from those in Swenson (2008).

Our results are also in contrast with those in Ma (2006), who finds that at the province level there is a positive correlation between total exports and exports of foreign firms. This study, however, is subject to a number of biases that we discussed in Chapter 1. More generally, literature on horizontal spillovers on exporting activity yields inconclusive results. Positive spillovers are found by Kneller and Pisu (2007) for the case of the United Kingdom and by Kokko, Zejan, and Tanzini (2001) for the case of Uruguay, while no such positive spillovers are found by Barrios, Görg, and Strobl (2003) for the case of Spain, and negative spillovers are found by Ruane and Sutherland (2005) for the case of Ireland. Our finding that horizontal FDI spillovers on exports vary by industry may shed light on these different findings — potential differences in industrial composition of different countries may lead to different patterns of spillovers on export activities.

5.1.2. Backward linkages

We now turn to the effects of foreign presence in downstream or upstream industries on the export share of domestic firms, where the downstream or upstream presence is computed using the input–output table as described in detail in Chapter 8. We begin by analyzing the effect of foreign presence in the industries downstream from domestic firms, which we refer to as spillovers through backward linkages. Once again, there are reasons to expect both positive and negative spillovers. We could expect positive effects because foreign-invested firms downstream may require an improved quality of inputs or even provide the blueprints for the inputs they require, which in turn could improve the competitiveness in foreign markets of the firms supplying these products. On the other hand, we could expect negative effects on foreign sales of these firms because there might be an increased demand domestically by foreign-invested firms for domestic firms' output, which may induce them to switch from exporting to supplying foreign-invested firms in their respective regions.

The results presented in Table 5.2 and Figure 5.3 show that, much like with horizontal spillovers, negative effects of FRN presence downstream are statistically significant for the full sample. Likewise, negative effects dominate for private firms, again only from FRN presence, while exports of state-owned firms are largely unaffected.

For specific industries, negative effects are found in industries producing predominantly intermediate inputs (paper, fuel processing, raw chemicals, rubber and metal products, industrial plastics, equipment, special

Table 5.2 Vertical spillovers from FDI on exports: Backward linkages.

Sector	L.HMT All dom.	L.FRN All dom.	Observations All dom.	Firms All dom.	L.HMT Private	L.FRN Private	Observations Private	Firms Private	L.HMT SOE	L.FRN SOE	Observations SOE	Firms SOE
Full Sample	-0.036	-0.067***	593892	230656	-0.053	-0.065*	249177	118902	-0.009	-0.017	59231	23647
Ferrous Metals	-0.070	-0.057	4644	2132	-0.084	-0.046	1817	1104	-0.011	-0.244	392	131
Nonferr. Metals	0.184	-0.697	4208	1785	0.146	-1.524	976	549	-0.118	0.063	735	316
Nonmetals	0.037	0.166	6531	2736	-0.921	1.203*	1814	1022	0.687***	0.328	1066	379
Agro-products	-0.113	-0.420*	40646	16596	-0.111	-0.210	15342	7680	-0.061	-0.350	6742	2901
Food	-0.180	-0.164	13173	5236	-0.420	-0.542**	4362	2177	0.216	-0.336	2329	979
Beverage	0.017	-0.155	10910	4164	0.149	-0.003	3451	1659	0.026	-0.040	2110	895
Textiles	-0.015	-0.163	53646	20747	-0.081	-0.304	28636	12933	0.149	0.275	2872	1234
Apparel	0.057	-0.036	19849	8152	0.298	0.259	10183	4938	0.033	0.622	592	248
Leather/Fur	0.058	-0.158	10493	4431	-0.068	-0.221	5988	2887	0.462	0.572	258	118
Timber	0.329**	0.228	11701	5307	0.364	0.239	5903	3113	0.063	-0.178	703	324
Furniture	0.568**	0.226*	5511	2340	0.576	0.303	2544	1314	-0.568**	-0.917	280	111
Paper	-0.071	-0.231***	21180	7681	-0.130	-0.319**	8475	3842	0.042	0.033	1271	515
Printing	0.006	-0.046	14312	5157	0.009	-0.151**	3989	1912	-0.137*	-0.115	4588	1585
Sports Goods	0.194	-0.109	4970	2087	0.340	0.233	2618	1247	-2.392	-0.720	195	84
Fuel Processing	-0.018***	0.019	4890	1994	0.015*	0.067	1698	902	0.003	-0.207	426	172
Raw Chemicals	-0.125*	-0.147**	47520	17653	-0.119**	-0.198****	18320	8631	0.031	-0.007	4916	1974
Pharmaceutical	-0.097*	-0.094*	14059	4908	-0.233	-0.170	4027	1878	0.215	0.268	1831	801
Chinese Meds.	-0.017	0.016	5449	2039	0.275	0.198	1465	715	0.004	0.141	758	368
Western Meds.	-0.077	-0.153*	7328	2703	-0.514*	-0.598**	2128	1026	0.335	0.295*	962	433

(Continued)

Table 5.2 (Continued)

Sector	L.HMT All dom.	L.FRN All dom.	Observations All dom.	Firms All dom.	L.HMT Private	L.FRN Private	Observations Private	Firms Private	L.HMT SOE	L.FRN SOE	Observations SOE	Firms SOE
Chemical Fiber	0.034	-0.015	2541	1010	0.050	-0.177	1328	632	-0.533	0.033	201	91
Rubber Prods.	-0.237**	-0.225*	6395	2423	-0.433***	-0.334**	2631	1238	-0.208	-0.379	447	181
Ind. Plastics	-0.029	-0.134**	13881	5759	0.032	-0.091	6269	3058	-0.266	0.140	780	355
Cons. Plastics	0.288**	0.108	9130	4127	0.330	0.090	4872	2518	-0.034	-0.012	251	112
Mineral Prods.	0.034	-0.057	63378	22596	-0.005	0.094	22816	10487	-0.060	-0.068	6766	2603
Ferr. Smelting	0.108	0.118	15806	6594	0.102	0.048	7124	3630	0.375	0.337	957	372
Nonferr. Smelt.	0.014	0.133	10598	4305	0.109	0.149	4469	2265	1.347***	0.582	639	270
Metal Prods.	-0.104***	-0.122***	28166	11578	-0.014	-0.068	12819	6319	0.082	-0.158	1200	515
Equipment	-0.098	-0.081*	44890	17269	-0.083	-0.009	21128	9798	-0.025	0.035	4164	1588
Spec. Equipment	-0.043	-0.113**	22222	8629	-0.180**	-0.120**	8909	4229	-0.083	-0.067	3615	1316
Transport	-0.028	-0.031	28303	10463	-0.152	-0.109	10543	4876	-0.077	-0.099*	4221	1630
Autos	-0.042	-0.023	15840	6219	-0.094	-0.084	6041	2952	-0.161	-0.106	2053	853
Electric Eq.	-0.112**	-0.109***	33322	12470	-0.172	-0.126	14143	6570	0.017	-0.016	2072	841
Electronics	-0.025	-0.024	10798	4316	-0.114***	-0.096***	4223	2057	-0.030	-0.031	1253	496
Telecom	-0.012	-0.006	1926	771	0.044	0.079	652	329	0.134	0.124	222	97
Computers	-0.150	-0.230	913	428	-0.173	-0.232*	303	178	0.627	0.277	90	44
Instruments	-0.037	-0.062	6167	2409	0.035	0.024	2573	1217	-0.071	-0.098	935	357
Handicraft	0.126	0.260	9061	3818	-0.276	-0.083	4753	2288	-0.521	-0.010	378	162

Dependent variable is export/output. All regressions include year dummies and control for firm fixed effects. RHS also includes log of number of employees, total debt as share of total assets, and firm age in years. Coefficients are not displayed for presentation purposes. Standard errors clustered on province and two-digit CIC sector code in parentheses; $^*p < 0.10$, $^{**}p < 0.05$, $^{***}p < 0.01$. Private firms defined as firms with majority individual share. State-owned enterprises (SOEs) defined as firms with majority state share.

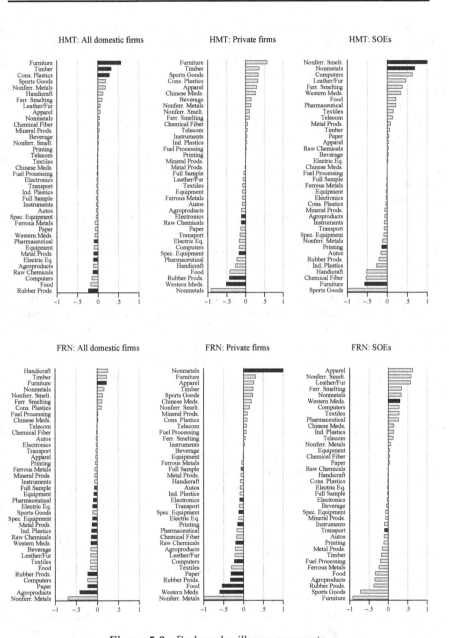

Figure 5.3 Backward spillovers on exports.
Note: Dark bars represent coefficients that are statistically significant at least at 10% level.

and electric equipment) as well as in industries producing consumer goods (pharmaceuticals and western medicine). Positive effects, however, are found in such important producers of intermediate inputs as firms in timber, furniture, and consumer plastics, but only for foreign capital from the Greater China Area. Additional negative backward FRN linkages are also observed for private firms in food, printing, electronics, and computers.

The negative effects of backward linkages observed for foreign investment suggest that the increasing demand from downstream foreign firms has siphoned domestic firms' products away from exports. Although there are positive productivity spillovers from downstream FDI that may increase domestic firms' competitiveness in the overseas market, such effects seem to be dominated by the diversion effect discussed above. Comparing the results in Chapter 3, we find that sectors that enjoy positive productivity backward linkages tend to not have negative export backward linkage effects. This is consistent with the two effects, increasing international competitiveness and diversion from export to domestic demand, go against each other.

Furthermore, the stronger negative effects of downstream presence of FRN on domestic firms' export suggest that firms with investment from outside of the Greater China Area may have established more supplier-client relations with domestic firms as compared to HMT-invested firms. These domestic firms, in turn, may have switched to supplying these foreign-invested firms instead of selling products abroad. In comparison, this effect does not dominate in the case of HMT capital.

5.1.3. Forward linkages

Table 5.3 and Figure 5.4 present the results from the analysis of forward linkages, which are the effects on domestic firms' exports of foreign presence in upstream industries. Higher quality and potentially cheaper inputs from foreign-invested firms upstream may make it easier for domestic firms to compete in foreign markets. At the same time, foreign-invested suppliers may divert their output from supplying domestic firms to supplying foreign-invested firms downstream or directly increase exports, thus cutting domestic firms out of the supply chain and making it more difficult for them to find intermediate inputs.

Again, we find predominantly negative effects that are consistent with the dominance of the latter mechanism described above. For example, as we know from Chapter 2, FDI increased exports of target firms in metal products and electric equipment industries. Since we measure exports as a proportion of total sales, this may imply that their output became less available to downstream firms located in China. Since these firms are suppliers to

Table 5.3 Vertical spillovers from FDI on exports: Forward linkages.

Sector	L.HMT All dom.	L.FRN All dom.	Observations All dom.	Firms All dom.	L.HMT Private	L.FRN Private	Observations Private	Firms Private	L.HMT SOE	L.FRN SOE	Observations SOE	Firms SOE
Full Sample	0.017	−0.034*	593892	230656	−0.024	−0.034	249177	118902	−0.004	−0.011	59231	23647
Ferrous Metals	−0.016	−0.014	4644	2132	−0.001	−0.014	1817	1104	−0.064	0.030	392	131
Nonferr. Metals	0.034	−0.122	4208	1785	0.135	−0.180	976	549	−0.006	−0.004	735	316
Nonmetals	0.153	0.009	6531	2736	−0.949	0.651	1814	1022	0.260	0.143	1066	379
Agro-products	−0.202	−0.595*	40646	16596	−0.174	−0.495*	15342	7680	0.017	−0.280	6742	2901
Food	−0.363	−0.415	13173	5236	−0.522	−0.762*	4362	2177	0.470	−0.720	2329	979
Beverage	−0.071	−0.203	10910	4164	−0.017	−0.150	3451	1659	−0.074	0.015	2110	895
Textiles	0.013	−0.122	53646	20747	−0.011	−0.216	28636	12933	0.201	0.098	2872	1234
Apparel	−0.035	−0.135	19849	8152	1.466	1.535	10183	4938	−2.443	−0.336	592	248
Leather/Fur	0.177	−0.623	10493	4431	−0.382	−1.056	5988	2887	0.407	1.198	258	118
Timber	0.458**	0.348*	11701	5307	0.431	0.356	5903	3113	0.268	−0.145	703	324
Furniture	0.790**	0.303*	5511	2340	0.865	0.450	2544	1314	−1.020**	−1.339	280	111
Paper	−0.075	−0.196***	21180	7681	−0.167	−0.297**	8475	3842	0.177	0.109	1271	515
Printing	−0.015	−0.058	14312	5157	0.016	−0.122	3989	1912	−0.147*	−0.127*	4588	1585
Sports Goods	0.100	−0.094	4970	2087	0.459	0.385	2618	1247	−0.903	−0.061	195	84
Fuel Processing	−0.047	−0.036	4890	1994	−0.069	−0.064	1698	902	0.084	−0.077	426	172
Raw Chemicals	−0.076	−0.092**	47520	17653	−0.099***	−0.123***	18320	8631	−0.022	−0.022	4916	1974
Pharmaceutical	−0.058	−0.057	14059	4908	−0.106	−0.073	4027	1878	0.223	0.302***	1831	801
Chinese Meds.	0.026	0.031	5449	2039	0.200	0.146	1465	715	−0.047	0.185	758	368
Western Meds.	−0.068	−0.103**	7328	2703	−0.269	−0.296	2128	1026	0.425***	0.333***	962	433

(*Continued*)

Table 5.3 (Continued)

Sector	L.HMT All dom.	L.FRN All dom.	Observations All dom.	Firms All dom.	L.HMT Private	L.FRN Private	Observations Private	Firms Private	L.HMT SOE	L.FRN SOE	Observations SOE	Firms SOE
Chemical Fiber	0.039	0.020	2541	1010	0.098	−0.011	1328	632	−0.416**	0.046	201	91
Rubber Prods.	−0.149**	−0.141*	6395	2423	−0.279***	−0.217**	2631	1238	−0.208	−0.251	447	181
Ind. Plastics	−0.056	−0.100***	13881	5759	−0.045	−0.083	6269	3058	−0.171	−0.073	780	355
Cons. Plastics	0.199	0.108	9130	4127	0.224	0.102	4872	2518	−0.021	−0.016	251	112
Mineral Prods.	−0.040	−0.077	63378	22596	−0.092	0.031	22816	10487	−0.033	−0.067	6766	2603
Ferr. Smelting	0.037	0.041	15806	6594	−0.008	−0.013	7124	3630	−0.021	0.089	957	372
Nonferr. Smelt.	0.023	0.049	10598	4305	0.090	0.078	4469	2265	0.156	0.081	639	270
Metal Prods.	−0.138***	−0.135***	28166	11578	−0.039	−0.078	12819	6319	−0.164	−0.384	1200	515
Equipment	−0.151**	−0.128**	44890	17269	−0.107	−0.029	21128	9798	0.005	0.078	4164	1588
Spec. Equipment	−0.073	−0.149**	22222	8629	−0.212*	−0.153*	8909	4229	−0.139	−0.103	3615	1316
Transport	−0.044	−0.039	28303	10463	−0.179	−0.131	10543	4876	−0.075	−0.120*	4221	1630
Autos	−0.073	−0.036	15840	6219	−0.148	−0.132	6041	2952	−0.245	−0.148	2053	853
Electric Eq.	−0.088*	−0.077*	33322	12470	−0.169*	−0.118	14143	6570	0.010	−0.018	2072	841
Electronics	−0.023	−0.024	10798	4316	−0.113***	−0.100**	4223	2057	−0.049	−0.053	1253	496
Telecom	−0.005	0.004	1926	771	0.052	0.095	652	329	0.107	0.103	222	97
Computers	−0.102	−0.204	913	428	−0.158	−0.221*	303	178	0.713	0.311	90	44
Instruments	−0.076	−0.116	6167	2409	−0.028	−0.024	2573	1217	−0.137	−0.235	935	357
Handicraft	0.209	0.333	9061	3818	−0.572	−0.208	4753	2288	−0.309	−0.190	378	162

Dependent variable is export/output. All regressions include year dummies and control for firm fixed effects. RHS also includes log of number of employees, total debt as share of total assets, and firm age in years. Coefficients are not displayed for presentation purposes. Standard errors clustered on province and two-digit CIC sector code in parentheses; $^* p < 0.10$, $^{**} p < 0.05$, $^{***} p < 0.01$. Private firms defined as firms with majority individual share. State-owned enterprises (SOEs) defined as firms with majority state share.

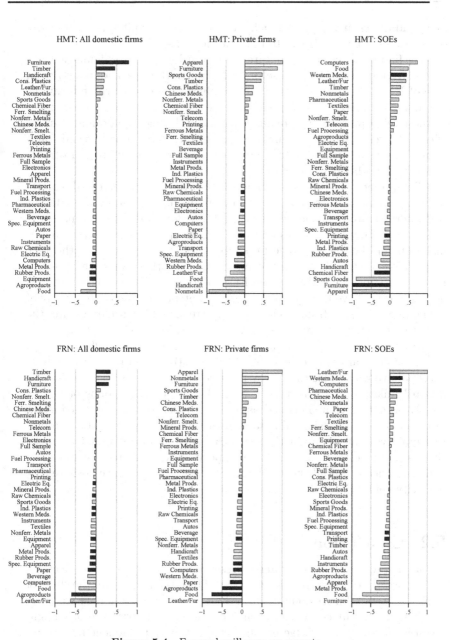

Figure 5.4 Forward spillovers on exports.

Note: Dark bars represent coefficients that are statistically significant at least at 10% level.

many industries, it may explain why we find negative spillovers, on average, of foreign presence upstream from domestic firms.

We find negative spillovers through forward linkages for domestic firms for many industries in the case of FRN, but only for a few industries in case of HMT. As before, most of the significant effects for the full sample are driven by private firms, while state-owned firms' exports do not react to the foreign presence upstream. For a few industries we do find positive effects of foreign firms upstream: timber and furniture industries and state-owned firms producing western medicine seem to benefit from upstream presence of both FRN and HMT.

The presence of FDI in upstream industries implies increased exports of foreign firms in these industries, thus reducing the supply of materials and intermediate parts needed for exports by domestic firms downstream. This is especially the case if domestic firms in upstream industries cannot make up for the gap in domestic supply, because they may be the very firms being bought by foreign capital. On the other hand, the positive productivity forward linkages from FDI observed in Chapter 3 suggest that domestic firms have become more efficient, potentially due to the supply of higher quality inputs from foreign firms upstream, which also dominates the higher cost factor. The findings above, however, indicate that the quantity reduction effect tends to dominate the quality improvement effect.

If we compare the sectors that have negative export forward linkage effects above with those that enjoy positive productivity spillovers through forward linkages (see Chapter 3), we find that the two groups of sectors mostly do not overlap. This is consistent with the two effects — reduction in the export market share due to competition with foreign firms' exports and improvement in productivity which increases international competitiveness in domestic firms — work in opposite directions, resulting in small and insignificant overall effect in industries that do experience positive productivity spillovers.

5.2. Conclusion

In this chapter we show that foreign presence had mostly negative effects on the exporting activities of domestic firms. Thus, the increase in the share of foreign sales by Chinese domestic firms that we see in the summary statistics in Chapter 1 occurred despite of, not because of, the presence of foreign-invested firms. The negative effects were especially prominent for private sector firms that experienced an increase in foreign direct investment from the Greater China Area in the same, upstream, or downstream industries. Exports of state-owned firms, by and large, do not seem to be much affected by the foreign presence, possibly because their foreign trading partners and logistics are well established. Nor are domestic firms affected by foreign investment from within the HMT region.

On the one hand, the overall picture painted in this chapter suggests the decreasing importance of domestic firms in Chinese exports, which is consistent with the increasingly higher percentage of total exports (and imports) accounted for by foreign-invested firms in the past decade (see, e.g., Naughton (2007)). Instead, Chinese domestic firms seem to have increasingly become the suppliers and customers of foreign-invested firms located in China, whereas the FDI firms increasingly get involved in producing exports. On the other hand, as our estimation specifications always control for time trends, any general growth in export over time has been captured that way. As a result, although the above pattern seems to suggest that Chinese domestic firms may have retreated from the export market, they in fact have more engagement in the global market (see Chapter 1 for evidence of higher share of total output sold abroad).

Thus, combined together, the above patterns show the increasingly deepened globalization in China, perhaps to a larger extent than commonly believed. Such globalization involves both the direct exporting behaviors of domestic firms and the supplier–customer relationships between domestic and foreign-invested firms in China. Given the increasing importance of supply chains involving both domestic and foreign firms in China, it is important to study the connection between exports and such supply chains in the future. And once again, these results, among other things, highlight the importance of analyzing spillover effects by industry, ownership type of the firm, and the source of foreign investment.

Chapter 6

FDI and the Incentives to Innovate and Imitate

The ability to design and develop new products determines the growth potential of a firm in the long run. Thus the impact of foreign capital on the innovation behaviors of domestic firms in the host country is of longer-term significance, as compared to FDI spillover effects on productivity, wages, and exports. Theoretically, the impact could be either positive or negative. On the one hand, if foreign-invested firms engage in more innovative behaviors, domestic firms may enjoy positive spillovers through learning or other interactions. Although our findings in Chapter 2 show no clear signs of foreign firms having a higher likelihood of producing more new products than domestic firms, still the presence of foreign-invested firms may prompt domestic firms to develop new products in order to face the increased competition, or to further reduce innovation in the attempt to cut costs (Aghion *et al.*, 2009). On the other hand, the inflow of FDI may lead to economic restructuring in China where domestic firms become an integral part of the global supply chain and thus produce to the specifications of foreign firms. In the process, they may lose the incentive to develop their own new products but rather resign to the role of producing mature products where lower production costs give them more advantage. And this effect may be important in both the horizontal FDI spillovers and the vertical FDI spillovers on innovation. In addition, it is also possible that imitation instead of original innovation has become more feasible given the presence of foreign firms and their readily available products. Thus, both the total amount of innovation and the relative importance of real innovation may drop in response to FDI inflow.

To better understand this issue, we study the spillover effects of FDI on domestic firms' innovation empirically in this chapter, against the background that in Chapter 2 we find no significant effects of foreign investment, positive or negative, on target firms' new product development. We begin by analyzing the overall effects of FDI presence on domestic firms' introduction of new products, and then go into depth to separate new product introduction into true innovation and imitation and study the separate FDI effects on these activities.

6.1. FDI Spillover Effects on New Product Introduction

To see how FDI presence impacts the introduction of new products by domestic firms, we use the 2000–2006 manufacturing census data (described in Chapter 8). The estimation method and specification used are similar to those adopted in the previous chapters and are discussed in detail in Chapter 8. Briefly, the dependent variable is a dummy variable indicating whether new product sales are positive in the firm in a certain year, and the main explanatory variable is the FDI presence measure constructed as usual. In addition, we control for firm and year fixed effects, as well as firm size measured by the log of the number of employees, firm age, and leverage (ratio of total debt to asset). In other specifications, we also drop leverage, or replace it with log of asset, and obtain very similar results.

6.1.1. Horizontal spillovers

By measuring the average FDI share of firms in the same industry (and the same province), we study the horizontal effects of FDI presence on new product introduction. Table 6.1 gives the estimation results for the whole sample of domestic firms, the private firm sample, and the SOE sample, which also allows differential effects for capital from within versus outside the Greater China Area. Figure 6.1 presents the graphic illustration of the same results.

In general, we find that the presence of FDI is associated with an overall significantly lower probability of having positive new product outputs. The pattern holds for both HMT and FRN, while the negative effect of FRN is larger and more prevalent across industries.

Aghion *et al.* (2009) make a theoretical argument and also provide evidence that increased competition is expected to discourage weak firms from innovating, but may stimulate innovative activity in firms that are competing "neck-to-neck" with their competitors in terms of technology. The predominantly negative impact of FDI presence shown in the table and the figure thus suggests that Chinese firms are relatively weak in comparison to their foreign competitors in the same industry (and province), especially when foreign investment comes from outside the Greater China Area. As discussed in the earlier chapters, firms invested by capital from these sources tend to have larger technology advantage compared to Chinese domestic firms. Furthermore, as shown in Chapter 2, there is no evidence that foreign

Table 6.1 Horizontal spillovers from FDI on new product sales.

Sector	L.HMT All dom.	L.FRN All dom.	Observations All dom.	Firms All dom.	L.HMT Private	L.FRN Private	Observations Private	Firms Private	L.HMT SOE	L.FRN SOE	Observations SOE	Firms SOE
Full Sample	-0.139*	-0.225***	590060	226624	-0.075	-0.156**	247134	117058	-0.052	-0.206***	61600	24327
Ferrous Metals	0.752	0.964	4669	2132	0.260	-0.682	1824	1104	-0.513	-0.328	401	137
Nonferr. Metals	-0.018	0.316	4187	1773	0.237	0.503	962	536	-0.022	0.373	754	327
Nonmetals	-0.006	-0.005	6520	2725	0.007	0.238	1809	1018	0.345	0.162	1092	390
Agroproducts	0.010	-0.308	40791	16495	0.210	-0.418*	15254	7580	0.019	0.021	7246	3089
Food	0.023	0.060	13197	5199	0.076	-0.016	4296	2129	-0.107	0.201	2538	1073
Beverage	0.137	0.110	10826	4098	0.027	-0.119	3414	1641	0.786***	0.427	2173	913
Textiles	0.055	-0.416	53325	20294	0.172	-0.414	28410	12715	-0.359	-1.094*	3120	1264
Apparel	0.073	-0.000	20010	7861	0.222	0.307	10291	4827	0.060	-0.049	648	256
Leather/Fur	-0.114	-0.296	10579	4336	-0.085	-0.302	6029	2853	0.143	0.154	309	139
Timber	0.277	0.115	11678	5255	1.106**	0.323	5882	3089	-0.069	-0.011	750	335
Furniture	0.323	-0.041	5447	2278	0.435	-0.012	2521	1290	0.200	0.729	295	115
Paper	-0.250	-0.233	21037	7574	-0.001	-0.167**	8381	3786	0.090	-0.048	1341	537
Printing	-0.190*	-0.400	14229	5097	-0.820***	-0.927***	3918	1875	0.062	-0.061	4700	1618
Sports Goods	0.176	0.135	4989	2008	0.136	0.153	2651	1214	-0.341**	-0.402**	212	92
Fuel Processing	-0.342*	0.236	4845	1965	-0.408***	-0.131	1684	890	-0.089	-0.361	435	175
Raw Chemicals	-0.520	-0.607	47035	17337	-0.327	-0.534	18064	8470	-0.952*	-0.635	5082	2022
Pharma-Ceutical	-0.594*	-0.600***	13650	4705	-0.858*	-0.788***	3949	1825	-1.303***	-0.829	1827	784
Chinese Meds.	-0.465	-0.210	5304	1966	-1.489**	-0.233	1440	695	-1.615**	-0.358	757	365
Western Meds.	-0.640	-0.798***	7090	2585	0.194	-0.845	2080	998	-1.116	-0.999	959	423

(Continued)

Table 6.1 (Continued)

Sector	L.HMT All dom.	L.FRN All dom.	Observations All dom.	Firms All dom.	L.HMT Private	L.FRN Private	Observations Private	Firms Private	L.HMT SOE	L.FRN SOE	Observations SOE	Firms SOE
Chemical Fiber	0.353*	0.074	2490	976	0.428*	−0.114	1303	615	0.200	1.143*	194	85
Rubber Prods.	−0.069	−0.057	6336	2376	−0.374	−0.309	2601	1222	0.509	0.648	474	185
Ind. Plastics	−0.113	−0.211*	13676	5638	−0.166	−0.288	6197	3010	−0.095	−0.009	795	362
Cons. Plastics	−0.228	−0.271	9015	4028	−0.391	−0.486	4827	2475	−0.298	−0.386**	255	112
Mineral Prods.	−1.458	−1.503	63003	22314	−0.728	−0.656	22615	10353	−0.748	−0.909	6958	2673
Ferr. Smelting	0.145	−0.290	15792	6570	0.212	−0.204	7109	3624	1.866**	0.315	1009	388
Nonferr. Smelt.	−0.013	−0.233*	10502	4239	−0.148	−0.297*	4422	2241	0.140	0.011	654	273
Metal Prods.	0.008	−0.122	28007	11393	−0.087	−0.218	12749	6243	−0.329**	−0.736**	1255	531
Equipment	−0.565	−0.461	44485	17012	−0.805	−0.539	20906	9644	−0.619	−0.557	4234	1601
Spec. Equipment	−0.400	−0.660*	22084	8522	−0.469	−0.968*	8806	4167	−0.583	−0.700**	3717	1345
Transport	−0.551	−0.373	28063	10283	−0.542	−0.612	10433	4810	0.102	0.188	4302	1636
Autos	−0.267	−0.209	15624	6098	−0.004	−0.105	5974	2912	0.629	−0.014	2057	847
Electric Eq.	−0.449*	−0.494*	32781	12133	−0.789**	−0.818**	13924	6425	−0.182	−0.377	2129	845
Electronics	−0.018	−0.100	10488	4109	0.021	−0.031	4124	1999	−0.201	−0.796**	1275	497
Telecom	0.110	0.168	1875	740	0.334	0.208	637	318	0.151	−0.617	225	100
Computers	0.122	−0.078	880	408	−0.551*	−0.510*	286	169	−0.157	−0.539	93	44
Instruments	−0.032	0.005	6142	2361	−0.257	−0.371	2544	1193	−0.253	0.132	963	360
Handicraft	−0.017	−0.450**	9222	3758	−0.127	−0.757***	4817	2266	0.278**	−0.139	415	177

Dependent variable is an indicator of a new product introduced. All regressions include year dummies and control for firm fixed effects. Controls include log of number of employees, total debt as share of total assets, and firm age in years. Coefficients are not displayed for presentation purposes. Standard errors clustered on province and two-digit CIC sector code in parentheses; *$p < 0.10$, **$p < 0.05$, ***$p < 0.01$.

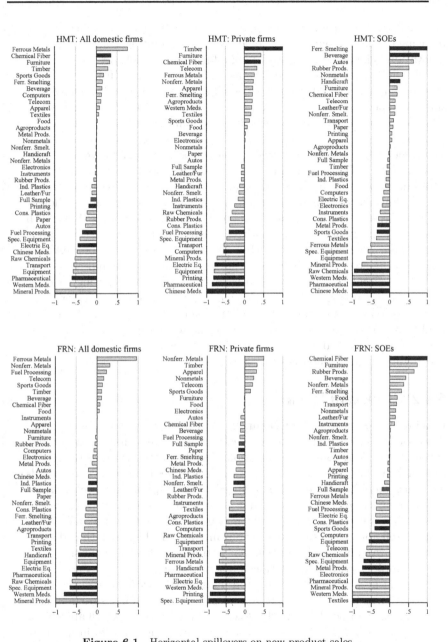

Figure 6.1 Horizontal spillovers on new product sales.
Note: Dark bars represent coefficients that are statistically significant at least at 10% level.

firms engage in more innovative activities relative to domestic firms, thus reducing the latter's opportunity of learning and imitating from the former's innovation behaviors when developing additional technologies.

We find that firms on average as well as firms in printing, fuel processing, pharmaceutical, western medicine, industrial plastics, nonferrous smelting, special equipment, electric equipment, and handicraft industries all suffer from negative horizontal spillovers from the presence of FDI on the probability that they will introduce new products. The only exception is the timber processing industry, which enjoys positive FDI spillovers — but recall that the FDI share in timber processing industry is very small. When domestic firms are split into private and SOEs, the above patterns largely persist, but the overall negative impact is significant only for spillovers from investment that is coming from outside the Greater China Area, with a few more industries showing positive horizontal spillovers of HMT presence. These differences between FRN and HMT are expected because of a greater technological gap between firms in mainland China and those outside of the Greater China Area and therefore a potential for tougher competition in innovation with firms invested by FRN capital. In addition, with the exception of handicraft, the industries suffering negative spillovers all tend to be capital-intensive sectors where the technology gap is the largest between domestic and foreign firms. Thus, the findings are consistent with the predictions in Aghion *et al.* (2009).

6.1.2. Backward linkages

In addition to the potential channels through learning and competition, domestic firms can also be affected by FDI in downstream industries through the supplier-client contracting relationship. By becoming the suppliers of foreign firms downstream, domestic firms' incentives to introduce new products may be either increased or reduced, depending on the foreign firms' decisions on production, export, and innovation. If foreign firms choose to focus on producing technologically mature goods at the most affordable costs to sell abroad, as suggested by our findings in Chapter 2, then domestic firms upstream may exhibit similar patterns in their behaviors.

To empirically test the relationship between foreign firm presence downstream and new product introduction by domestic firms, we use the same specification as in the section above, except that the FDI measure used here is the average of FDI shares in the downstream industries (see Chapter 8 for details). Table 6.2 and Figure 6.2 show the estimation results in numbers and in graphs, respectively.

The observed effects of backward linkages of FDI on new product sales are negative and significant for foreign capital from all geographic regions,

Sector	L.HMT All dom.	L.FRN All dom.	Observations All dom.	Firms All dom.	L.HMT Private	L.FRN Private	Observations Private	Firms Private	L.HMT SOE	L.FRN SOE	Observations SOE	Firms SOE
Full Sample	-0.301^{**}	-0.413^{***}	590060	226624	-0.259^{**}	-0.343^{***}	247134	117058	-0.245^{*}	-0.609^{***}	61600	24327
Ferrous Metals	-1.111	-0.706	4669	2132	-2.754	-1.466	1824	1104	-0.218	-0.299	401	137
Nonferr. Metals	-1.287	-0.269	4187	1773	-3.963	-2.730^{*}	962	536	-1.269	1.530^{**}	754	327
Nonmetals	-0.119	-0.652	6520	2725	-0.104	0.568	1809	1018	1.190	1.216	1092	390
Agropro-ducts	-1.440	-1.616	40791	16495	-1.307	-1.520^{*}	15254	7580	-0.633	-1.047	7246	3089
Food	-0.683	-0.912	13197	5199	-1.209	-1.287	4296	2129	-0.384	-0.224	2538	1073
Beverage	-0.762	-0.970	10826	4098	-0.072	-1.121	3414	1641	-0.876	-1.502	2173	913
Textiles	-0.481	-0.806^{*}	53325	20294	-0.793	-1.030^{**}	28410	12715	-0.450	-1.502^{**}	3120	1264
Apparel	-0.255	-0.376	20010	7861	-0.435	-0.437	10291	4827	0.082	0.121	648	256
Leather/Fur	-0.261	-0.506	10579	4336	-0.552	-1.048^{*}	6029	2853	-0.467	-1.241	309	139
Timber	-0.072	-0.541	11678	5255	0.667	-0.263	5882	3089	0.086	-0.113	750	335
Furniture	0.292	-0.273	5447	2278	0.906	0.361	2521	1290	1.021	-0.272	295	115
Paper	-0.491	-0.761	21037	7574	0.232	-0.168	8381	3786	1.165^{***}	-0.467	1341	537
Printing	-0.388	-0.412	14229	5097	-0.857	-0.779	3918	1875	-0.142	-0.282	4700	1618
Sports Goods	0.184	0.127	4989	2008	-0.751	-0.605	2651	1214	-1.737^{**}	-1.277	212	92
Fuel Processing	0.020	-0.542^{*}	4845	1965	-0.046	-0.494	1684	890	0.028	-0.465	435	175
Raw Chemicals	-0.626	-0.738^{*}	47035	17337	-0.541	-0.682^{*}	18064	8470	-1.104	-1.108^{**}	5082	2022
Pharma-ceutical	-0.566	-0.837^{*}	13650	4705	-1.938^{***}	-1.782^{***}	3949	1825	-0.751	-0.933	1827	784
Chinese Meds.	-0.848^{*}	-0.909	5304	1966	-1.883	-2.368^{**}	1440	695	-0.507	-1.029	757	365
Western Meds.	-0.660	-0.910^{*}	7090	2585	-2.178^{**}	-1.314	2080	998	-1.206	-1.026	959	423

(Continued)

Table 6.2 (*Continued*)

Sector	L.HMT All dom.	L.FRN All dom.	Observations All dom.	Firms All dom.	L.HMT Private	L.FRN Private	Observations Private	Firms Private	L.HMT SOE	L.FRN SOE	Observations SOE	Firms SOE
Chemical Fiber	-1.205***	-0.729*	2490	976	-0.747	-0.333	1303	615	2.049	2.689*	194	85
Rubber Prods.	-0.023	-0.276	6336	2376	-0.526	-0.571	2601	1222	-0.221	-0.264	474	185
Ind. Plastics	-0.264	-0.444**	13676	5638	-0.306	-0.634*	6197	3010	-0.307	-0.488	795	362
Cons. Plastics	-0.283	-0.343	9015	4028	-0.460	-0.660	4827	2475	-0.592	0.214	255	112
Mineral Prods.	-0.902	-1.069	63003	22314	-0.793	-0.645	22615	10353	-0.451	-0.552	6958	2673
Ferr. Smelting	-0.351	-0.557*	15792	6570	-0.145	-0.533	7109	3624	0.697	-0.694	1009	388
Nonferr. Smelt.	-0.623	-0.429	10502	4239	-1.030	-0.503	4422	2241	0.161	-0.576	654	273
Metal Prods.	-0.226	-0.221	28007	11393	-0.570	-0.465	12749	6243	0.247	-0.415	1255	531
Equipment	-0.596	-0.633*	44485	17012	-1.076**	-0.906**	20906	9644	-0.033	-0.535	4234	1601
Spec. Equip-ment	-0.752	-0.799**	22084	8522	-1.299**	-1.103**	8806	4167	-0.516	-1.194**	3717	1345
Transport	-0.579*	-0.611**	28063	10283	-0.648	-0.800*	10433	4810	-0.211	0.026	4302	1636
Autos	-0.292	-0.303	15624	6098	-0.413	-0.452	5974	2912	-0.081	-0.015	2057	847
Electric Eq.	-0.584*	-0.568*	32781	12133	-0.888*	-0.815*	13924	6425	-0.139	-0.550	2129	845
Electronics	-0.079	-0.162	10488	4109	-0.035	-0.104	4124	1999	-0.214	-0.749***	1275	497
Telecom	-0.038	-0.022	1875	740	0.248	0.011	637	318	0.195	-0.449	225	100
Computers	0.106	-0.108	880	408	-0.490	-0.450	286	169	-0.546	-0.749	93	44
Instruments	0.009	-0.059	6142	2361	-0.160	-0.261	2544	1193	-0.492	-0.339	963	360
Handicraft	0.332	-0.510	9222	3758	0.732	-0.345	4817	2266	0.400*	-0.522	415	177

Dependent variable is an indicator of a new product introduced. All regressions include year dummies and control for firm fixed effects. Controls include log of number of employees, total debt as share of total assets, and firm age in years. Coefficients are not displayed for presentation purposes. Standard errors clustered on province and two-digit CIC sector code in parentheses; $*p < 0.10$, $**p < 0.05$, $***p < 0.01$.

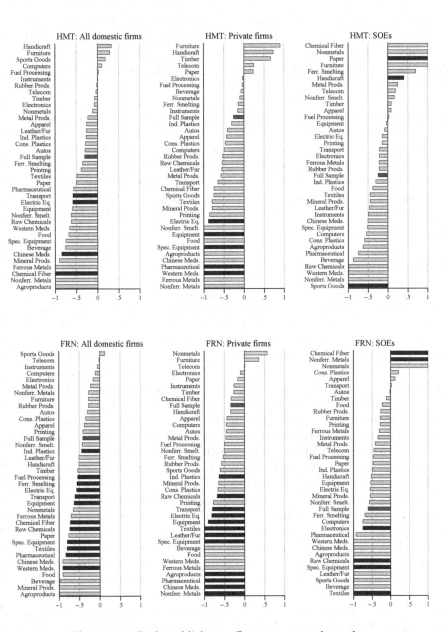

Figure 6.2 Backward linkages effects on new product sales.
Note: Dark bars represent coefficients that are statistically significant at least at 10% level.

although the negative effect is larger for FRN than for HMT. And such negative impact is also significant for both private domestic firms as well as SOEs. At the specific industry level, a wide range of industries suffer from the negative FDI spillovers, including fuel processing, raw chemicals, pharmaceutical, western medicine, industrial plastics, ferrous and nonferrous smelting, and various kinds of equipment. Most of the industries fall into the category of producers of raw materials and intermediate goods. Thus the patterns are consistent with foreign firms using existing products of domestic firms as their inputs rather than requesting new inputs to be produced by their Chinese suppliers. Another potential explanation relates to findings in the previous chapters. The positive backward spillovers of FDI on domestic firms' productivity may have increased their profit margins high enough so that they have lost the motivation for further innovation.

6.1.3. Forward linkages

The other direction in which FDI could exert vertical spillovers on domestic firms is through foreign firms' client relationship. By investing in the producers of raw materials and intermediary goods, foreign firms can influence the supplies to domestic firms, thus impact their innovation decisions. Such spillovers can be driven either by quality of inputs and intermediate products that is likely to improve with foreign presence in upstream industries, or by prices of inputs and intermediate products that can either increase or fall depending on the marketing strategy or productivity impacts of foreign investment in upstream industries. In particular, even more standardized inputs of better quality produced by foreign-invested firms, which is a common channel for productivity improvement, may have dampening effects on domestic firms' innovative behaviors. This counterintuitive effect is due to the fact that domestic firms are less motivated to develop new processes or products, given the readily available product and production standards. Once again, only empirical tests can give clear answers as to the direction of the effects.

Table 6.3 and Figure 6.3 show the estimation results in numbers and in graphs, respectively. The results are very similar to those observed for backward linkages, with negative and significant effects of upstream FDI presence on domestic firms' new product sales. In Chapter 2, we find higher productivity of foreign firms, and in Chapter 3 we find positive forward linkages of FDI presence on domestic firms' productivity. Thus the most plausible explanation for the results in Table 6.3 and Figure 6.3 is that the lower prices of inputs produced by foreign firms as well as the higher productivity of domestic firms downstream have resulted in fewer incentives

Table 6.3 Vertical spillovers from FDI on new product sales: Forward linkages.

Sector	L.HMT All dom.	L.FRN All dom.	Observations All dom.	Firms All dom.	L.HMT Private	L.FRN Private	Observations Private	Firms Private	L.HMT SOE	L.FRN SOE	Observations SOE	Firms SOE
Full Sample	-0.320^{***}	-0.370^{***}	590060	226624	-0.263^{**}	-0.313^{***}	247134	117058	-0.213^{*}	-0.527^{***}	61600	24327
Ferrous Metals	-0.141	-0.288	4669	2132	-0.352	-0.376	1824	1104	0.046	-0.376^{*}	401	137
Nonferr. Metals	-0.172	-0.148	4187	1773	-0.173	-0.744	962	536	-0.050	0.157	754	327
Nonmetals	-0.097	-0.693	6520	2725	-0.162	0.615	1809	1018	1.168	0.603	1092	390
Agropro-ducts	-1.903	-2.225	40791	16495	-1.427	-1.987	15254	7580	-0.996	-1.572	7246	3089
Food	-1.074	-1.337	13197	5199	-1.411	-1.575	4296	2129	-1.047	-0.760	2538	1073
Beverage	-0.840	-1.303	10826	4098	0.436	-1.469	3414	1641	-0.920	-1.957	2173	913
Textiles	-0.187	-0.478	53325	20294	-0.234	-0.490	28410	12715	-0.297	-1.491^{*}	3120	1264
Apparel	-1.164	-1.216	20010	7861	-1.235	-1.011	10291	4827	0.326	0.080	648	256
Leather/Fur	-0.192	-1.176	10579	4336	-0.679	-2.388	6029	2853	0.131	-2.931	309	139
Timber	0.314	-0.476	11678	5255	1.541	-0.022	5882	3089	0.318	0.059	750	335
Furniture	0.718	-0.114	5447	2278	1.503	0.697	2521	1290	1.342	0.065	295	115
Paper	-0.520	-0.736	21037	7574	0.192	-0.164	8381	3786	1.055^{**}	-0.513	1341	537
Printing	-0.419	-0.427	14229	5097	-0.720	-0.709	3918	1875	-0.122	-0.240	4700	1618
Sports Goods	-0.004	-0.077	4989	2008	-0.936^{*}	-0.863	2651	1214	-0.995	-0.609	212	92
Fuel Processing	-0.384	-0.474	4845	1965	-0.868^{**}	-0.714^{**}	1684	890	-0.035	-0.054	435	175
Raw Chemicals	-0.446	-0.471^{*}	47035	17337	-0.235	-0.339	18064	8470	-0.913^{**}	-0.905^{**}	5082	2022
Pharma-ceutical	-0.508	-0.557^{**}	13650	4705	-1.356^{***}	-1.156^{***}	3949	1825	-1.178^{***}	-0.912^{**}	1827	784
Chinese Meds.	-0.792^{*}	-0.732^{*}	5304	1966	-1.544	-1.790^{**}	1440	695	-1.067^{***}	-0.889^{*}	757	365
Western Meds.	-0.591^{*}	-0.591^{**}	7090	2585	-1.264^{**}	-0.695	2080	998	-1.244^{*}	-0.916	959	423

(Continued)

Table 6.3 (*Continued*)

Sector	L.HMT All dom.	L.FRN All dom.	Observations All dom.	Firms All dom.	L.HMT Private	L.FRN Private	Observations Private	Firms Private	L.HMT SOE	L.FRN SOE	Observations SOE	Firms SOE
Chemical Fiber	-0.730**	-0.504**	2490	976	-0.406	-0.236	1303	615	0.749	1.667	194	85
Rubber Prods.	-0.055	-0.170	6336	2376	-0.163	-0.171	2601	1222	-1.096	-1.064	474	185
Ind. Plastics	-0.097	-0.210	13676	5638	-0.091	-0.277	6197	3010	-0.064	-0.244	795	362
Cons. Plastics	-0.061	-0.119	9015	4028	-0.093	-0.238	4827	2475	0.143	0.391	255	112
Mineral Prods.	-0.955	-0.992	63003	22314	-0.429	-0.428	22615	10353	-0.732	-0.666	6958	2673
Ferr. Smelting	-0.181	-0.271*	15792	6570	-0.128	-0.214	7109	3624	1.124**	-0.626	1009	388
Nonferr. Smelt.	-0.517	-0.387	10502	4239	-0.710*	-0.497*	4422	2241	-0.517	-0.511	654	273
Metal Prods.	-0.390	-0.335	28007	11393	-0.790**	-0.690**	12749	6243	0.110	-0.384	1255	531
Equipment	-0.892	-0.918*	44485	17012	-1.394**	-1.231**	20906	9644	-0.230	-0.667	4234	1601
Spec. Equipment	-1.229*	-1.250**	22084	8522	-1.877***	-1.706***	8806	4167	-1.061	-1.486**	3717	1345
Transport	-0.990*	-0.904**	28063	10283	-0.970	-1.116	10433	4810	-0.035	0.172	4302	1636
Autos	-0.496	-0.449	15624	6098	-0.451	-0.502	5974	2912	0.343	0.011	2057	847
Electric Eq.	-0.546*	-0.499*	32781	12133	-0.685*	-0.669*	13924	6425	-0.482	-0.508	2129	845
Electronics	-0.061	-0.152	10488	4109	-0.003	-0.081	4124	1999	-0.229	-0.806**	1275	497
Telecom	0.020	0.050	1875	740	0.322	0.095	637	318	0.126	-0.586	225	100
Computers	0.162	-0.058	880	408	-0.580	-0.542	286	169	-0.179	-0.478	93	44
Instruments	0.051	-0.105	6142	2361	-0.533	-0.663	2544	1193	-1.202	-1.066	963	360
Handicraft	0.214	-0.830	9222	3758	0.823	-0.580	4817	2266	0.969**	-0.133	415	177

Dependent variable is an indicator of a new product introduced. All regressions include year dummies and control for firm fixed effects. Controls include log of number of employees, total debt as share of total assets, and firm age in years. Coefficients are not displayed for presentation purposes. Standard errors clustered on province and two-digit CIC sector code in parentheses; $p < 0.10$, $**p < 0.05$, $***p < 0.01$.

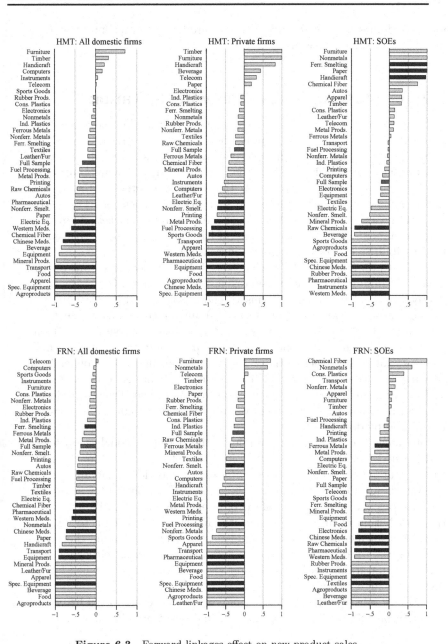

Figure 6.3 Forward linkages effect on new product sales.
Note: Dark bars represent coefficients that are statistically significant at least at 10%
level.

for these domestic firms to introduce new products, as their profit margins may have already increased enough.

6.2. Comparing Innovation with Imitation

So far we have focused on the overall effects of FDI on domestic firms' new product introduction. Unfortunately, the NBS manufacturing census data set we have been working with so far does not allow us to tell whether these new products were truly novel for the markets or merely new products for the firm but imitations of products that already existed on the market. In the remainder of this chapter we separate the effects of FDI on true innovation versus imitation of existing products on the market and propose a new channel for this particular kind of FDI spillovers — an expansion in the possibilities of vertical product differentiation.[1]

To better understand the mechanisms of these spillovers, we first develop a partial equilibrium model of heterogeneous firms that differ in their productivity and allow domestic firms to choose between three alternatives: (a) not introduce any new products, (b) introduce a new product line (innovate), or (c) develop a variety that is a very close substitute to an existing product line developed by another firm (imitate). There is a fixed cost associated with each activity and the equilibrium choice depends on the firm's relative productivity. The presence of foreign firms generates spillovers via increased returns to imitation, as foreign firms introduce a range of products that consumers value more highly than the innovations introduced by domestic firms.

To focus on the empirical findings, the detailed model is presented and discussed in the appendix section of this chapter. An important feature of our model is the various empirical implications that allow us to separate innovation and imitation effects of FDI. In particular, under the assumptions of our model, the effects of foreign presence are different across the distribution of firms. We expect the increase in imitation to be most prominent for medium-sized less-sophisticated firms that would choose not to introduce a new variety in the absence of foreign firms, either by innovation or imitation, but that do enter the imitation market when foreign presence is high enough.

We test whether the predictions of our model are supported by using a combination of firm surveys that include measures of new product

---

[1]Parts of this analysis appeared in *Scandinavian Journal of Economics* in an article coauthored with Irene Brambilla (Brambilla, Hale, and Long, 2009).

introduction and firm characteristics, and merge these data with measures of foreign presence at the industry level constructed from the manufacturing census. China presents a perfect case study to analyze this empirical question, because it received enormous inflows of FDI and, especially, of R&D FDI in the past decade (Huggins, Demirbag, and Ratcheva, 2007).

6.2.1. Empirical analysis

We now turn to the empirical analysis to see whether we find systematic evidence of an increase in FDI leading to an increase in "new" product introduction in the Chinese manufacturing sector. We rely on the richness of the firm-level survey data to analyze various types of firms and distinguish between the effects of FDI on imitation and innovation activities by domestic firms.

A combination of two sources of data are used in the analysis. At the firm level, we use data from the World Bank's 2001 and 2003 Investment Climate Surveys. A total of 1500 firms were interviewed during the first survey in five Chinese cities in 2001. The second survey was run in 2003 and included 2400 firms in 18 different cities. These surveys are described in detail in Chapter 8.

The main survey variable that describes the creation of new product variety is a binary variable that indicates whether a firm introduced any new product in a given year. As defined in the survey, a new product is a variety that was not previously produced by a given firm, independently of whether a similar variety already existed in the market. In addition to the binary variable, the surveys provide information on the total number of goods introduced. Unfortunately, firms only report the total number of goods introduced over the whole survey period instead of on a yearly basis. The binary variable, on the other hand, is reported on a yearly basis and thus allows us to exploit the panel nature of the data, which is crucial for our analysis.

The definition of what constitutes a new variety is essentially subjective to the firm; it can refer to a new production line or to the refurbishing of an existing product. However, this subjectivity will not bias the results as long as it is uncorrelated with foreign presence in each industry.

Our second data set includes information on presence of foreign firms at the industry level. We define foreign presence as the share of foreign firms in total industry output, where foreign firms are weighted by their percentage of foreign ownership. The output data have been collected by the China National Bureau of Statistics (NBS) at the firm level and then aggregated up to 600 industries, based on the four-digit Chinese Industrial Classification. Our sample covers the period of 1998 to 2001.[2]

The first and second sources of data can be matched at the industry level. Since we have no foreign-firm output data available for the year 2002, the last year of the 2003 firm survey is not exploited in the analysis. We have three years of data for firms in the first survey (1998–2000) and two years of data for firms in the second survey (2000–2001).

This combination of firm-level and industry-level data allows for a rich economic analysis. The firm survey provides information on firm characteristics that are not available in studies using census data. The industry data allows for consistent and precise measures of foreign presence, as the variables are constructed from large samples of firms that are representative of the manufacturing sector. Most studies of the effects of FDI on domestic firms are based either on firm surveys from which both the firm-level variables and the composition of the industry are derived, or by census-like data set that does not contain much information about the firms.

6.2.2. Estimation results

Our model predicts that as more foreign firms enter and introduce new products available for imitation, more domestic firms that did not choose to introduce new products before will now choose to imitate, while some of the firms that chose to introduce new products (innovate), will now choose instead to imitate existing products. This is because the return to innovation falls while return to imitation increases. Overall, with a larger foreign presence, we would expect that more firms introduce new products of some kind, and that this overall increase comes from less productive unsophisticated firms that did not introduce new products in the past.

Table 6.4 reports the results of our basic regressions for the effects of FDI presence on new product introduction. In all specifications we include firm and year-fixed effects and control for nonparallel trends across firms by including interactions of a linear trend with three different labor quality variables as described in Table 6.4. The results show that, in the first specification, an FDI presence of 24% (the mean across industries in the sample) is associated with an increase in the probability of introducing a new product of 26 percentage points: The share of FDI presence is defined as a number between 0 and 100. Results in all other specifications are virtually identical.

---

[2]We are grateful to Mary Amiti and Beata Javorcik, who generously provided these data. See Amiti and Javorcik (2008) for a more detailed description of the data source and measures.

Table 6.4 FDI and product introduction.

	(1)	(2)	(3)	(4)
Foreign presence	0.011**	0.011**	0.011**	0.0096*
	(0.0051)	(0.0053)	(0.0051)	(0.0052)
Trend*R&D workers	−0.0073	−0.0073	−0.0076	—
	(0.013)	(0.014)	(0.013)	
Trend*Nonprod. workers	—	0.0011	—	—
		(0.0042)		
Trend*Education	—	—	−0.0031	—
			(0.026)	
Firms	1027	981	1027	1052
Obs.	2390	2278	2390	2457
R^2	0.05	0.05	0.05	0.05

Sample: private domestic firms. Dependent variable: binary variable indicating the introduction of new products. Foreign presence: participation of foreign firms in industry output. Trend*R&D workers: linear trend interacted with the initial share of R&D workers in skilled workers. Trend*Non-prod. workers: linear trend interacted with initial share of non-production workers. Trend*Education: linear trend interacted with an indicator of whether the average education level is middle school or high school. Other controls (not displayed): firm fixed effects and year effects. Industry-clustered standard errors in parenthesis; *significant at 10%; **significant at 5%; ***significant at 1%.

Evidence from heterogeneous firms as support of the imitation hypothesis

We next turn to analyzing how the effect of FDI presence on new product introduction differs across firms of different types. The model is highly stylized and only allows for one dimension of heterogeneity in firms (underlying productivity, which has a one-to-one correspondence with firm size). But in the empirical analysis, we consider several variables that indicate the degree of "sophistication" of a firm. These results are reported in Tables 6.5–6.7 and they all support the imitation hypothesis whereby foreign presence generates positive spillovers on less sophisticated firms.

Table 6.5 presents our results with respect to firm size measured as the number of employees or as the firm's market share, and the firm's exporting status. In the top panel we split our sample into small, medium, and large firms according to their number of employees (below 50, between 50 and 150, and above 150). We find that the effect of FDI presence on new product introduction is *only* present in medium-sized firms. This is consistent with our model: While the largest firms always introduce new products,

Table 6.5 Differential effects by firm characteristics.

Size (number of workers)[a]	Small	Medium	Large
Foreign presence	0.008	0.025**	0.0021
	(0.010)	(0.013)	(0.0052)
Firms	284	315	428
Obs.	668	718	1004
R^2	0.11	0.08	0.03

Market share (self-reported)	Below 5%	Above 5%
Foreign presence	0.014***	0.0073
	(0.0054)	(0.0099)
Firms	685	342
Obs.	1528	862
R^2	0.06	0.05

Exporting status	Nonexporters	Exporters
Foreign presence	0.016**	0.0003
	(0.0075)	(0.0051)
Firms	727	294
Obs.	1651	726
R^2	0.06	0.06

Sample: private domestic firms. Dependent variable: binary variable indicating the introduction of new products. Foreign presence: participation of foreign firms in industry output. Other controls (not displayed): firm fixed effects, year effects, and firm-level trends in initial R&D activity (measured as the ratio of R&D workers over the total number of skilled workers). Industry-clustered standard errors in parenthesis; *significant at 10%; **significant at 5%; ***significant at 1%.
[a]Small: less than 50 employees; Medium: 50–150 employees; Large: more than 150 employees.

the increase in FDI presence will likely make them partially switch from innovation to imitation, but not necessarily increase the frequency of new product introduction. The smallest firms might be too small to even afford the expense of imitating. The medium-sized firms, however, who are not able to innovate, find it easier to introduce new products under FDI presence because imitation becomes more profitable. Thus an increase in FDI presence in their sector is likely to increase the frequency of new product introduction in these domestic firms. We also note that the magnitude of the effect more than doubles when the sample is not diluted by the firms that do not experience the effect of FDI presence (compared to the results for the full sample reported in Table 6.4, the effect of a 1% increase in foreign presence jumps from 1.1 to 2.5 percentage points increase in the probability of introducing a new product).

The middle panel reports the results separately for firms with small and with large market shares. We find, again consistent with our model, that the effect of FDI presence on product introduction is fully concentrated in small firms — those with less than 5% market share (as self-declared in the survey). The intuition for this result is that firms with market power (high market share) can benefit from innovation whether or not they compete with foreign firms in their industry, while firms without market power would not choose to innovate, but would increase their propensity to introduce new products through imitation when FDI presence is higher.

The bottom panel reports results separately for firms that do and that do not export (again as self-reported in the survey and cross-checked with another survey entry on the share of foreign sales). We find that the increase in product introduction due to FDI presence is concentrated among non-exporters. This is consistent with the imitation effect of FDI that we conjectured, because exporters are bound by reputation and international agreements on foreign markets and cannot as easily get away with imitation — it is common knowledge that Chinese pirated goods are much easier to get in China.

Next, in Table 6.6, we look at characteristics related to the workforce composition, capital intensity, and equipment sophistication of firms that are more likely to introduce new products when FDI presence in their sector increases. We show that the effect of FDI on new product introduction is concentrated among firms with higher share of unskilled workers (approximated with the share of production workers), with lower education level of the workforce (approximated as the average education level of production workers), with lower capital to labor ratio, and with no imported machinery. In other words, firms that have introduced new products are more likely to be imitators than to be innovators.

Another way to look at the sophistication of firms is to look at their R&D expenses and the quality of their products. Table 6.7 reports the results. We find that only for the subsample of medium-sized firms, having positive R&D expenses is associated with the increase in new product introduction as a result of higher FDI presence. This is consistent with the conjecture that even imitation requires some R&D expenditure, while supporting the hypothesis that the increase in imitation is concentrated among medium-sized firms. In the third panel, we exploit data on R&D workers. We find that spillovers from FDI are concentrated among firms with lower share of R&D scientists over the total number of R&D workers. Furthermore, firms without ISO9000-certified products increase their probability of introducing new products in face of higher FDI presence, while firms that have ISO9000 certification do not. These results once again confirm our hypothesis that the new product introduction brought about by higher FDI

Table 6.6 Skill intensity, capital intensity and equipment.

Share of non-production workers in total employment	Below the sector mean	Above the sector mean
Foreign presence	0.014**	0.0044
	(0.0065)	(0.0076)
Firms	726	255
Obs.	1686	592
R^2	0.06	0.06

Average education of production workers	Middle school	High school
Foreign presence	0.015**	0.0024
	(0.0062)	(0.0079)
Firms	405	622
Obs.	1146	1244
R^2	0.06	0.05

Capital per worker	Below the sector mean	Above the sector mean
Foreign presence	0.023**	−0.0001
	(0.011)	(0.0056)
Firms	465	461
Obs.	1056	1061
R^2	0.06	0.03

Imported machinery	No	Yes
Foreign presence	0.015**	0.0013
	(0.0075)	(0.0058)
Firms	690	318
Obs.	1596	756
R^2	0.07	0.05

Sample: private domestic firms. Dependent variable: binary variable indicating the introduction of new products. Foreign presence: participation of foreign firms in industry output. Other controls (not displayed): firm fixed effects, year effects, and firm-level trends in initial R&D activity (measured as the ratio of R&D workers over the total number of skilled workers). Industry-clustered standard errors in parenthesis; *significant at 10%; **significant at 5%; ***significant at 1%.

is not due to true innovation but is driven by increased imitation of existing products.

Additional results

Table 6.8 displays results from regressions where the left-hand side variable is the ratio of R&D expenditure to sales, computed for the full sample

Table 6.7 R&D and product quality.

R&D expenditure	Zero	Positive
Foreign presence	0.0075	0.0067
	(0.0076)	(0.0077)
Firms	559	371
Obs.	1265	860
R^2	0.06	0.02

R&D expenditure; Medium-sized firms	Zero	Positive
Foreign presence	0.021	0.032**
	(0.014)	(0.016)
Firms	205	101
Obs.	468	230
R^2	0.11	0.09

R&D scientists/R&D workers	Below the sector mean	Above the sector mean
Foreign presence	0.015**	0.0071
	(0.0074)	(0.0075)
Firms	628	399
Obs.	1474	916
R^2	0.08	0.02

Certified products (ISO9000)	No	Yes
Foreign presence	0.018**	0.0057
	(0.0073)	(0.007)
Firms	520	486
Obs.	1196	1131
R^2	0.06	0.06

Sample: private domestic firms. Dependent variable: binary variable indicating the introduction of new products. Foreign presence: participation of foreign firms in industry output. Other controls (not displayed): firm fixed effects, year effects, and firm-level trends in initial R&D activity (measured as the ratio of R&D workers over the total number of skilled workers). Industry-clustered standard errors in parenthesis; *significant at 10%; **significant at 5%; ***significant at 1%.

as well as three groups of firms by size (small, medium, and large). We do not find a statistically significant effect of foreign presence on R&D expenditure by firms in the full sample or in our subsamples, regardless of specification and sample used. These results are, however, broadly consistent with the model. If we interpret the difference between fixed costs of imitation and innovation as additional R&D required, an increase in FDI would lead to an increase in R&D expenditure for firms that did

Table 6.8 Effects of FDI on expenditure in R&D.

	All	Small	Medium	Large
Foreign presence	0.029	−0.0014	0.0841	−0.002
	(0.030)	(0.0017)	(0.0817)	(0.0031)
Firms	1007	276	311	420
Obs.	2232	557	699	976
R^2	0.003	0.0192	0.00757	0.0306

Sample: private domestic firms. Dependent variable: expenditure in R&D over firm sales. Foreign presence: participation of foreign firms in industry output. Other controls (not displayed): firm fixed effects, year effects, and firm-level trends in initial R&D activity (measured as the ratio of R&D workers over the total number of skilled workers). Industry-clustered standard errors in parenthesis; *significant at 10%; **significant at 5%; ***significant at 1%.

not introduce any new products before and to a decline in R&D expenditure for firms that switch from innovation to imitation. Thus, the effect of increased FDI presence on the average R&D expenditure is ambiguous, which is consistent with the lack of effects for the full sample shown in column one. The results for subsamples of large- and medium-sized firms are also consistent with the model in that they are of the right sign and their magnitude is non-negligible. The lack of statistical significance could be partly due to the high variance in R&D expenditure across firms, exacerbated by the use of fixed effects and the small sample size. In addition to true differences in R&D expenditures across firms, there is also likely a measurement error due to lax regulation on what expenses are attributed to R&D expenditure.

In Table 6.9 we report the results of our regressions of product introduction according to whether firms engage in commercial transactions with foreign firms. The survey asks firms several questions about the nature of their commercial relationships with foreign firms which allow us to identify domestic firms that are suppliers or clients of foreign firms. The questions are whether the domestic firm produces final products, parts or inputs for foreign firms (either of its own designed or following provided blueprints), and whether it uses parts supplied by foreign firms. There are, however, many missing values, which limits our sample substantially. Nevertheless, we consistently find that firms that *do not* have relationships with foreign firms are more likely to introduce new products when FDI presence is higher. This result would be inconsistent with the technology transfer hypothesis in which foreign firms make it easier for domestic firms to innovate, because in this case firms with closer ties to foreign firms would be more likely to benefit. This result, however, is quite consistent

Table 6.9 Commercial transactions with foreign firms located in China.

Produces final products for foreign firms?	No	Yes
Foreign presence	0.021**	−0.0052
	(0.0088)	(0.0088)
Firms	257	67
Obs.	771	201
R^2	0.08	0.05
Produces parts or inputs for foreign firms?	No	Yes
Foreign presence	0.020**	0.002
	(0.008)	(0.013)
Firms	263	63
Obs.	789	189
R^2	0.08	0.09
To the specifications of foreign firms?	No	Yes
Foreign presence	0.019**	0.0097
	(0.0087)	(0.0069)
Firms	202	124
Obs.	606	372
R^2	0.07	0.07
Of its own design?	No	Yes
Foreign presence	0.018***	−0.021
	(0.0067)	(0.016)
Firms	262	49
Obs.	786	147
R^2	0.07	0.06
Uses parts supplied by foreign firms?	No	Yes
Foreign presence	0.022***	−0.0036
	(0.0077)	(0.011)
Firms	214	106
Obs.	642	316
R^2	0.09	0.03

Sample: private domestic firms. Dependent variable: binary variable indicating the introduction of new products. Foreign presence: participation of foreign firms in industry output. Other controls (not displayed): firm fixed effects, year fixed effects, and firm-level trends in initial R&D activity (measured as the ratio of R&D workers over the total number of skilled workers). Industry-clustered standard errors in parenthesis; *significant at 10%; **significant at 5%; ***significant at 1%.

with the imitation hypothesis — firms that produce or design goods or materials for foreign firms or use their parts would be more hesitant to imitate, fearing repercussions, while firms without such ties find it beneficial to imitate products brought in by FDI.

6.3. Conclusion

To sum up, we show that the recent surge in FDI flows to China is not a likely source of upgrading in China's domestic innovation activities. On the one hand, FDI presence has negative rather than positive overall effects on domestic firms' new product sales. On the other hand, when FDI presence does lead to new product introduction, it is likely to lower incentives for true innovation and increase incentives for imitation. In fact, it is the less sophisticated firms that increase the frequency of new (to them) product introduction when FDI presence in their sector rises.

The analysis based on the NBS manufacturing census shows negative overall spillovers on new product sales, while the World Bank data analysis shows some positive effects of FDI presence on new product introduction. Several factors can explain the differences. First, the FDI measure in the NBS analysis is constructed at the industry-province level, thus limiting the spillover effects to a narrower "sphere of influence," as compared to the study using the World Bank data, where the FDI measure is computed at the industry level. Given that there may be more domestic firms with higher original technology level when all firms in the same industry are included, it is then more likely to observe positive effects on innovation in the study using World Bank data (Aghion *et al.*, 2009). Second, the World Bank data include a larger number of small- and medium-sized firms, which may find the imitation option more attractive at the presence of FDI. This then makes it more likely to find positive FDI spillovers on new product sales in the study of the World Bank data set.

However, both studies are consistent in showing that interactions through supplier or client relationship with foreign firms lead to lower likelihood of new product introduction. Among the findings based on the NBS census data, FDI presence in downstream or upstream industries has particularly large negative spillover effects on domestic firms' new product introduction (Tables 6.2 and 6.3). Similarly, the study using the World Bank data shows that domestic firms with direct contracting relationships with foreign firms are less likely to report new product development, as compared to other domestic firms (Table 6.9).

6.4. Appendix A: Model of FDI Spillovers on Innovation and Imitation

In this section, we describe the theoretical model that underlies the empirical findings above. In the model we outline demand-related channels for spillovers from foreign firms to domestic firms in the decision to introduce new products. The model is static and contemplates only one time period. We integrate a firm's dynamic decision to introduce a new product into a static framework by modeling it as a one-time decision to upgrade quality. When firms enter the market, they are "assigned" a baseline quality-differentiated variety. By paying fixed costs of R&D, firms can choose to upgrade their variety to a higher-quality one, either by creating a new product or by imitating an existing product, as explained in more detail below. In this sense, product introduction is not viewed as a horizontal expansion in the range of products, but as a progression up the quality ladder as in Grossman and Helpman (1991a, b).

The externality channel that we describe is related to consumers' preferences and thus requires structure on the utility function. We start by describing a benchmark case with a nested CES utility function and products that are vertically as well as horizontally differentiated. Goods produced by foreign firms are introduced at a later stage.

The higher-level utility function is defined over composite products as

$$U = \left(Q_0^{\frac{\theta-1}{\theta}} + \int_0^N Q_i^{\frac{\theta-1}{\theta}} di \right)^{\frac{\theta}{\theta-1}}, \qquad (6.1)$$

where $\theta > 1$ is the elasticity of substitution. Each product is a composition of n_i varieties of different quality γ indexed by v that are aggregated with constant elasticity of substitution as well. All baseline-quality varieties (with quality normalized to one) are grouped in product "zero," which is defined as

$$Q_0 = \underbrace{\left(\int_0^{n_0} q_v^{\frac{\sigma-1}{\sigma}} dv \right)^{\frac{\sigma}{\sigma-1}}}_{\text{baseline varieties}}. \qquad (6.2)$$

The parameter σ satisfies the restriction $\sigma > \theta > 1$, so that the elasticity of substitution between varieties of the same product is larger than the elasticity of substitution across products.

All other products indexed $i > 0$ are compositions of upgraded, higher-quality, varieties defined as

$$Q_i = \left(\gamma_2 q_{\text{original}}^{\frac{\sigma-1}{\sigma}} + \underbrace{\int_0^{n_i} \gamma_1 q_v^{\frac{\sigma-1}{\sigma}} dv}_{\text{imitations}} \right)^{\frac{\sigma}{\sigma-1}} ; \quad i \in (0, N]. \qquad (6.3)$$

Here we distinguish between two types of varieties: the original variety and the imitations (indexed from 0 to n_i). Consumers value original varieties more highly than imitations, which in turn are valued more highly than baseline-quality varieties in group zero, i.e., $\gamma_2 > \gamma_1 > 1$. This assumption can also be interpreted as a static short-hand for a dynamic model in which the producer of the original variety enjoys one period of monopoly profits before imitations become available. It can also be interpreted as additional value that consumers attach to brand-name products.

We can derive the demand for variety v as a function of its own price and quality (γ), the quality-corrected group price index, the overall price index, and exogenous income (see the on-line Appendix available at the author's websites for equations for the price indexes and demand function). The exogeneity of income is a partial equilibrium simplification whereby wages are not determined within the model. The model could be easily extended to a multi-industry setting by adding another layer to the utility function and a homogeneous good sector that under simplifying assumptions would pin down wages, as it is often assumed in the differentiated products literature. These extensions, however, would not add wage effects to the model.

On the supply side, firms are heterogeneous as in Melitz (2003), with an exogenous distribution of production costs per unit ($1/\psi$) described by a cdf $G(\psi)$. There is a fixed mass of firms, M, that enter the market at the same time and learn their unit production cost (or inverse productivity) upon entry. The number of firms in the end of the period, however, is endogenous, due to exit of the least productive firms. One way to think about the "no entry" assumption, is to assume that in a dynamic version of the model each new firm has to spend one period producing a standard-quality product zero. Allowing entry into this category would not change the implications of the model. For simplicity, we assume that there is no entry at all.

Each firm produces only one variety. Once they have learnt their productivity ψ, firms can choose to either exit, stay and produce the existing baseline-quality-assigned variety (by paying a fixed cost of production F_0), stay and imitate an existing higher-quality variety (by paying $F_0 + F_1$), or stay and create an original higher-quality product line (by paying $F_0 + F_2$, with $F_2 > F_1$). Firms that choose to imitate are randomly assigned to a product group in the range $(0, N]$.

We make the standard monopolistic competition assumption that firms compete in prices and are small relative to the market. To simplify matters we further assume that the number of groups is small relative to the number of firms, so that each firm, including the innovator, is small within a given group.[3] In practice, this assumption means that the price of one firm exerts

---

[3]The number of groups is an endogenous variable. The primitive assumption is that the fixed cost of creating an original product line is sufficiently high.

no influence on the market price index and on the group price index and it yields the standard constant mark-up result $p_v = \sigma/(\sigma - 1)1/\psi_v$. The random assignment to product groups implies that with a large number of firms the equilibrium distribution of imitators is the same across product groups — with the exception of group zero, where by definition there are no imitators — and in particular that the number of imitated varieties is the same across groups ($n_i = n$).

Given the optimal price decision above, we can solve the firm problem backwards and find the optimal decision for production, imitation and innovation. For this purpose we need to compare total profits under four alternatives: exit, no upgrades (denoted by 0), imitation (denoted by 1), and innovation (denoted by 2). Firms that choose to exit earn zero profits. To find profits (optimized over prices) of the alternatives that imply staying in the market, we plug the price solution into the variable profit function and subtract the fixed costs of production, imitation or innovation. Let those profits be denoted by V_0, V_1, and V_2, defined as

$$V_0(\psi) = k\psi^{\sigma-1}P_0^{\sigma-\theta}\Pi^{\theta-1} - F_0 \qquad \text{(no upgrades)},$$

$$V_1(\psi) = k\gamma_1^{\sigma}\psi^{\sigma-1}P^{\sigma-\theta}\Pi^{\theta-1} - F_0 - F_1 \quad \text{(imitation)}, \qquad (6.4)$$

$$V_2(\psi) = k\gamma_2^{\sigma}\psi^{\sigma-1}P^{\sigma-\theta}\Pi^{\theta-1} - F_0 - F_2 \quad \text{(innovation)},$$

with $k = (\sigma - 1)^{\sigma-1}/\sigma^{\sigma}y$. The variables P_0, P, Π, and y are the group price index for product zero, the group price index for all other products, the overall price index, and the exogenous nominal income.

It should be noted that technically the price index for groups $i > 0$ is not the same across groups because of differences in productivity, and equilibrium prices, across innovators (the distribution of imitators, on the other hand, is the same across groups if the number of firms is large enough). Since by assumption all firms are small, including the innovators, the contribution of the innovators to the group price indexes are negligible and can be disregarded, which means that price indexes are approximately the same across groups. Alternatively, we could define P as the expected price index before an imitator is assigned to a group, $P = E(P_i \,|\, i > 0)$. The former assumption, however, makes the algebra much more tractable in the case with foreign firms that we discuss in the next subsection.

The options to exit, produce at baseline-quality, imitate or innovate imply incurring different fixed costs and earning variable profits that are increasing in the productivity level ψ. The result is a sorting on ψ as in Melitz (2003) and Helpman, Melitz, and Yeaple (2004). It is possible to add more dimensions of firm heterogeneity such as efficiency in R&D or in quality provision as in Brambilla (2009) and Hallak and Sivadasan (2006). In this particular setting, however, given that we focus on demand channels for spillovers, a richer description of the technology would not add to the analysis. Intuitively, the higher quality options have higher fixed costs and yield higher variable profits. As productivity increases, firms expand sales and take advantage of higher variable profits more easily. Thus, firms with highest productivity will profit from the highest fixed-cost option.

We can define cutoff values of productivity ψ that allow us to sort firms according to their choices. We denote those cutoffs by ψ_0, ψ_1, and ψ_2. Firms with productivity below ψ_0 choose to exit; firms with productivity between ψ_0 and ψ_1 keep the default baseline-quality; firms with productivity between ψ_1 and ψ_2 upgrade by imitation and get randomly assigned to a group $i > 0$; finally, firms with productivity above ψ_2 upgrade by innovation. These assumptions on the model primitives are needed to obtain a positive number of firms in each group (Melitz, 2003; Helpman, Melitz, and Yeaple, 2004). The cutoffs are analytically defined as $V_0(\psi_0) = 0$, $V_1(\psi_1) = V_0(\psi_1)$, $V_2(\psi_2) = V_1(\psi_2)$; and yield the results

$$\psi_0 = \left(\frac{F_0}{kP_0^{\sigma-\theta}\Pi^{\theta-1}} \right)^{\frac{1}{(\sigma-1)}}, \tag{6.5}$$

$$\psi_1 = \left(\frac{F_1}{k\Pi^{\theta-1}(P^{\sigma-\theta}\gamma_1^{\sigma} - P_0^{\sigma-\theta})} \right)^{\frac{1}{(\sigma-1)}}, \tag{6.6}$$

$$\psi_2 = \left(\frac{F_2 - F_1}{kP^{\sigma-\theta}\Pi^{\theta-1}(\gamma_2^{\sigma} - \gamma_1^{\sigma})} \right)^{\frac{1}{(1-\sigma)}}. \tag{6.7}$$

The system of Eqs. (6.5)–(6.7), together with the definitions of the price indexes (see Appendix) can be solved to obtain the equilibrium cutoffs and price indexes. There are $n_0 = [G(\psi_1) - G(\psi_0)]M$ firms that choose not to upgrade and produce the baseline-quality varieties in product zero; there are N upgraded product lines (indexed by $i \in (0, N]$) created by $N = [1 - G(\psi_2)]M$ firms that innovate; and there are $[G(\psi_2) - G(\psi_1)]M$ firms, randomly assigned across groups $i \in (0, N]$, that upgrade by imitation.

Figure 6.4 depicts the equilibrium in Panel A. Net profits from each alternative are plotted as a function of productivity. The solid dots denote the productivity cutoffs. Firms between the origin and the first dot choose to exit; firms between the first two dots stay and do not introduce upgrades; firms between the second two dots imitate; and firms above the third dot innovate. The sorting occurs because the options with the higher fixed costs (measured in the vertical axis) are at the same time the options with higher gross profits per unit (measured by the slope of V).

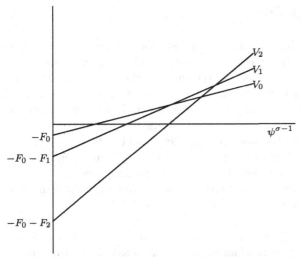

Panel A: Domestic Firms. Net profits from not upgrading, imitation, and innovation are plotted as a function of productivity. The solid dots denote the productivity cutoffs. Firms between the origin and the first dot choose to exit; firms between the first two dots stay and do not introduce upgrades; firms between the second two dots choose to imitate; and firms above the third dot choose to innovate.

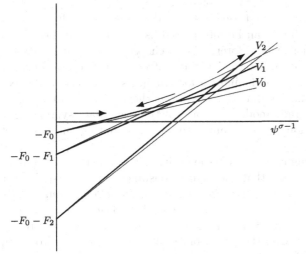

Panel B: Change in Profits due to Foreign Firms. The figure depicts a shift in net profits and cutoffs due to an increase in M^*/M. The thick lines and solid dots denote the original situation. The thin lines and empty circles denote an increase in M^*/M. The slope of V_0 and V_2 decreases, while the slope of V_1 increases. The arrows indicate the direction in which the cutoffs shift.

Figure 6.4   Profits from not upgrading, imitation, and innovation.

A.1. Foreign firms

We now introduce foreign firms into the model. Foreign firms are also heterogeneous and their productivity distribution, fixed costs of production, imitation and innovation are the same as those of domestic firms. To keep the model simple and consistent with the assumptions for domestic firms, we abstract from international general equilibrium effects and focus on a case with a fixed number of foreign firms M^*. We further assume that foreign firms enter the domestic market if and only if they innovate. As a result, we have a number $N^* = (1 - G(\psi_2)) M^*$ of foreign firms that enter the domestic market and introduce N^* original innovations. Since foreign and domestic firms are symmetric, the fraction of original innovations that are of foreign origin is given by $M^*/(M + M^*)$.

The product lines introduced by foreign firms are vertically differentiated from the product lines introduced by domestic firms. Anecdotal evidence suggests that multinationals are often associated with the production of higher quality goods. Additionally, multinationals often have significant brand-name recognition. Further, they usually spend significant amounts on advertising. Our assumption is that consumers value product groups introduced by multinationals more highly than product lines introduced by domestic firms — by a factor of $1 < \delta < \gamma_2/\gamma_1$.

In equilibrium, imitation activity depends positively on the value of δ. The parameter δ can be interpreted as a reduced form coefficient from a richer problem where foreign firms choose their optimal degree of vertical differentiation internalizing its effect on imitation. The possibility of being imitated could induce foreign firms to choose a degree of vertical differentiation that is lower than the optimum. In a context of a North–South trade model, Taylor (1994) shows that asymmetric property rights protection prevents innovators from adopting the best technology available.

The parameter δ enters in the utility function in the same way as γ_1 and γ_2. We also assume that the higher consumer valuation spills over to the imitators in the same group. Advertising could be one channel for valuation spillovers. When foreign firms advertise their own variety, consumers also become more aware of the varieties in the same product group. This valuation spillover raises the profitability of imitation relative to no upgrades and to innovation.

Domestic firms have the same choices as in the benchmark case with no foreign firms: exit, produce a baseline-quality variety in group zero, imitate a high-quality product, or introduce an original high-quality product. Imitators get randomly assigned to product groups, with a probability $M^*/(M + M^*)$ of being assigned to a group of foreign origin. The profits of not upgrading, imitation, and innovation can be redefined as

$$V_0(\psi) = k\psi^{\sigma-1}P_0^{\sigma-\theta}\Pi^{\theta-1} - F_0,$$

$$V_1(\psi) = k\gamma_1^\sigma\psi^{\sigma-1}P^{\sigma-\theta}\Pi^{\theta-1}f\left(\frac{M^*}{M}\right) - F_0 - F_1, \qquad (6.8)$$

$$V_2(\psi) = k\gamma_2^\sigma\psi^{\sigma-1}P^{\sigma-\theta}\Pi^{\theta-1} - F_0 - F_2,$$

with $f(M^*/M) = (M + \delta^{(\sigma\frac{\theta-1}{\sigma-1})}M^*)/(M + M^*)$.

The presence of foreign firms affects the profitability of domestic firms through three channels. First, the main spillover channel is an increase in the valuation of the domestic varieties introduced by firms that imitate products of foreign origin, from γ_1 to $\delta\gamma_1$. This implies an increase in expected benefits from imitation. At the same time, we have that the higher consumer valuation brings down the price index in foreign groups, which acts in the opposite direction, reducing expected profits. The net effect is positive. Algebraically, the net increase in expected profits from imitation is captured by the term $f(M^*/M)$, which depends positively on the share of foreign firms in the total number of firms.

Second, there are changes in price indexes that affect the profitability of the three alternatives (no upgrades, imitation, and innovation). The overall price index is affected by vertical differentiation. A fraction $M^*/(M + M^*)$ of the upgraded product groups (those of foreign origin) are vertically differentiated by a factor δ. The overall price index Π is redefined taking the vertical differentiation given by δ into consideration (see on-line Appendix). The overall price index is decreasing in the share of foreign firms (due to the increase in consumer valuation), which implies a decrease in profits for the three alternatives. At the same time, the group price indexes for upgraded products (foreign and domestic) goes up reflecting an increase in the number of groups and a decrease in competition within groups; however, the negative vertical differentiation effect of the overall price index is dominant provided vertical differentiation (δ) and substitution between groups (θ) are high enough.

Summing up, we have that the three alternatives (no upgrades, imitation, and innovation) become less profitable relative to exit, because of a decrease in the overall price index. In addition, we have that the relative profitability of imitation goes up because of the probability of being assigned to a higher valuation group. It can be shown that the net effect on the profits from imitation is positive. As a result, we find that as the ratio of foreign firms (M^*/M) increases, the cutoffs ψ_0 and ψ_2 increase, while ψ_1 decreases.

Finally, there is a second-order effect whereby all price indexes change due to changes in the cutoffs ψ_0, ψ_1, and ψ_2. In fact, price indexes and the cutoffs are jointly determined in equilibrium.

Figure 6.4 depicts an increase in M^*/M in Panel B. The slopes of V_0 and V_2 decrease, reflecting the negative effect of the overall price index. These two options become relatively less profitable. At the same time, the slope of V_1 increases due to the positive consumer valuation effect that dominates the negative group price index effect and overall price index effect. As a result, we find that the range of firms that chooses to imitate increases at the expense of firms that innovate, but also at the expense of firms that were not introducing upgrades before — the cutoffs ψ_2 and ψ_1 move to the right and left respectively. There is also an increase in exit.

In this analysis we assume that $\delta < \gamma_2/\gamma_1$, that is, consumers value domestic innovations more highly than imitation of foreign varieties. The effects of FDI on domestic innovation and imitation are larger, the higher the value of δ — as when δ is higher when the expected profits from imitation are larger. In the extreme, if $\delta > \gamma_2/\gamma_1$, there is no domestic innovation.

Chapter 7

Conclusion

In the previous chapters, we have studied the multiple aspects of FDI impacts on China. In this chapter, we summarize the findings and suggest some new directions for future research on FDI in general.

As shown in Chapter 1, Figure 1.1, the overall level of FDI inflow into China rose from almost nonexistence gradually until the late 1980s, when the pace slowed down due to the Tiananmen Square incident. It then picked up speed after 1992, the year of Mr. Deng Xiaoping's Southern Tour, which revived economic reforms in China. This was followed by healthy growth in the volume of FDI in the second half of the 1990s, followed by another round of rapid growth since 2002, when China ascended to the World Trade Organization (WTO). This pattern is consistent with the Chinese government's policies toward FDI, which were first initiated in the early 1980s as part of the opening up of the special economic zones (SEZs), the original four being Shenzhen, Shantou, Xiamen, and Zhuhai. The further opening up to foreign capital in the mid-1990s of all major cities along the east coast as well as along the Yangtze River and the Yellow River greatly expanded opportunities for foreign investors in China. Leading to China's ascension to the WTO, domestic laws and government policies were drafted or changed to give foreign investors access to more sectors in the Chinese economy. These policy developments are very much reflected in the patterns of overall FDI inflow into China since the early 1980s. Figure 1.2 further indicates two patterns in the recent development of FDI inflow into China: First, the sectoral distribution of foreign direct investment into China has switched from mainly focusing on labor-intensive industries to targeting both capital-intensive industries and labor-intensive industries. Second, while FDI from the Hong Kong, Macao, and Taiwan continue to grow, FDI from regions outside the Greater China Area grew even more rapidly.

Despite the long period of fast growth of FDI and the good prospect for its further expansion, empirical studies have not produced convincing evidence that FDI has positively impacted Chinese domestic firms. The current book attempts to better address these issues and to provide additional findings. We also look at a wider set of performance measures, study both direct and spillover effects of FDI, as well as explore these effects at a more disaggregated level.

As we use multiple data sets and also choose separately the estimation strategy that most suits the features of each data set, we devote Chapter 8 to describe the data sets as well as the most appropriate empirical method corresponding to each of the issues studied and the data sets used. Briefly, we use two data sets, the Chinese Manufacturing Survey of Large- and Medium-Sized Firms conducted by the National Bureau of Statistics between 2000 and 2006 (the NBS census data) and the World Bank Business Environment Surveys of 2001 and 2003 (the WB data). The NBS data set includes a huge number of firms, with a large proportion of them included for multiple years. As a result, we mostly use panel data methods to analyze the data set (such as the system GMM method). The WB surveys were conducted only in 2001 and 2003 for non-overlapping sets of firms, thus the majority of variables have values only for one year and we are therefore confined to using methods designed for cross-sectional data sets. For some variables, retrospective values were requested for up to three years in the WB data, and we use panel analysis to study those variables.

Our main analysis begins in Chapter 2, where we explore the direct effects of FDI on the target firms in China from multiple perspectives. In terms of total factor productivity (TFP), we find that the TFP of the target firms on average is positively correlated with the percentage of company shares that are foreign-owned. Yet there is a substantial amount of variation among firms in the FDI effects on their TFP. Different effects are observed in different sectors, and FDI from outside of the Greater China Area tends to have more positive spillovers on firm productivity.

We also use the NBS census data to compare foreign-invested firms with domestic firms in wages, exports, and new product sales, after controlling for other firm characteristics. Consistent with conventional beliefs, foreign-invested firms tend to pay higher wages, while firms with HMT investment also export a higher proportion of their output. Yet contrary to the common belief, we do not find clear evidence that foreign-invested firms are more likely to have positive new product sales. In addition, the wage differential is surprisingly small in magnitude. However, the lack of significant FDI effects on unskilled labor wage that we find using the World Bank firm survey helps to explain the small magnitude of the overall FDI effect on average wage.

The World Bank data set provides more detailed information on employee characteristics, which allows us to control for labor quality when studying FDI effects on wages. When using this data set, we observe that foreign-invested firms tend to hire younger employees, whether they are production workers, engineers, or managers. They also tend to hire managers with more education and more experience with other foreign firms. In terms of wages, they pay a premium to engineers and managers but not to production workers, and these results hold even after controlling for age, education, and foreign firm working experience of the employees.

These results suggest that foreign-invested firms in China indeed are able to benefit from the ample availability of cheap unskilled workers, at least until shortly before 2001, when the World Bank survey was conducted. On the other hand, the relatively inelastic supply of skilled labor (labor with technical or managerial expertise) and the higher productivity in foreign firms have led to higher wages for skilled labor in foreign-invested firms. These results imply that FDI presence did potentially drive up wages for skilled workers but has not yet exerted an upward pressure on wages for unskilled labor at this point in time.

Starting with Chapter 3, we investigate the indirect or spillover effects of FDI presence on domestic firms. The focus of Chapter 3 is on TFP. Overall, several patterns have emerged from our study of FDI spillovers on TFP. First of all, there are more positive vertical spillovers from FDI presence than horizontal spillovers, suggesting that within-industry competition between foreign-invested firms and domestic firms does seem important in the host country. Secondly, Chinese private domestic firms are more likely to enjoy both positive horizontal spillover effects as well as positive backward and forward FDI spillovers, as compared to their SOE counterparts, which on average do not experience significant within-industry spillovers and suffer negative backward and forward FDI spillovers from FRN investment. Thirdly, there is evidence that compared to FDI from Hong Kong, Macao, and Taiwan, foreign capital from other parts of the world brings more positive spillovers to Chinese domestic firms, but also has greater negative impact on Chinese SOEs. The variations across firm ownership types and FDI origins again point to the importance of disaggregated studies.

Chapter 4 presents the findings based on the WB survey data relating employee wages and quality to FDI presence, and the findings further highlight the different FDI effects on Chinese domestic firms of different ownership types. While Chinese private firms begin with paying higher wages, hiring younger-aged employees in all categories, as well as employing engineers and managers with more education and more foreign-firm experience (but less educated production workers) as compared to their SOE counterparts, they are able to obtain engineers and managers with even more education and foreign-firm experience in the presence of FDI. This seems to suggest that the presence of FDI has attracted more technical and managerial talents into the region, which leads to potential positive labor market spillover effects for domestic firms. On the other hand, private domestic firms do need to pay substantially higher wages to their engineers and managers when there are foreign-invested firms close by (in the same industry and city), implying that foreign presence drives up wages for skilled labor in the local market, which is a competition effect with a potentially negative impact on domestic firms' profitability. In fact, this potential negative impact of FDI in the labor market becomes very real for Chinese SOEs, which have to pay substantially higher wages to their engineers and managers in the presence of FDI in the same industry and city. The quality of their skilled labor, however, remains the same or even deteriorates (although the change is not always statistically significant). Thus, in addition to increased product market competition, FDI presence may exert another negative effect on domestic firms in the host country by driving up their operating costs.

Exports are another important area where FDI presence potentially impacts Chinese domestic firms, a topic we turn to in Chapter 5. Contrary to the generally positive FDI effects on the TFP of domestic firms, the average effect of FDI from outside the HMT region on their export performance is negative! Furthermore, the negative spillovers hold regardless of whether the FRN investment is made in the same industry or in the downstream or upstream industries.

This appears contradictory to the findings in Swenson (2008), which show that domestic private firms are more likely to explore new export destinations or to develop new products for export when they have more contact with foreign-invested exporters. Swenson interprets the findings as supporting evidence for the positive impact of FDI presence on domestic firms' export performance through information spillovers. Yet since the author does not look at the total value of exports by domestic firms, these findings are also consistent with an alternative explanation, which leads to a less sanguine conclusion on foreign firms' role in affecting domestic firms' exports. It is just as likely that domestic firms have shifted to new export products or destinations, precisely because they have been negatively impacted in the existing export markets due to increased competition from foreign-invested firms. Thus without looking at the overall effects on total exports of domestic firms, it is impossible to evaluate whether FDI presence plays a positive or negative role in promoting export performance of domestic firms. In fact, the findings in Chapter 5 show that the overall spillover effects of FDI presence on domestic firms' export volume are negative.

Because of the strong positive effects of foreign investment on the exports of target firms themselves, the total impact of FDI on Chinese exports still tends to be positive. On the one hand, the negative spillovers on domestic firms' exports may point to the potential negative impact of FDI on indigenous firms. Yet on the other hand, these findings are also consistent with a deeper involvement of Chinese domestic firms in the globalization process. These firms may have shifted from directly exporting to overseas markets to supplying products to foreign-invested firms in China. The findings made in Chapter 5 suggest that foreign investment from outside the Greater China Area has played a more important' role in developing such supply chains in China.

In Chapter 6, we use both the NBS census data and the World Bank survey data to explore the last but also potentially the most important aspect of firm performance affected by FDI presence, i.e., the innovation behaviors of domestic firms. Here, the message is also complex. Results from the NBS data analysis show a negative overall impact of FDI on domestic firms' likelihood of new product sales, regardless of the industry.

The patterns emerging from the World Bank data are more subtle. On one hand, private domestic firms in China have a higher likelihood of developing new products when they have more exposure to FDI presence, i.e. a higher output share by foreign-invested firms in the same industry. On the other hand, the characteristics of the Chinese private firms that develop new products in the presence of FDI suggest something peculiar about these "new" products. Contrary to expectations, when FDI is present, it is the medium-sized non-exporters with low market shares that report new product development between 2000 and 2003. In addition, the firms that develop new products also tend to have less educated production workers, lower proportions of skilled labor among their employees, as well as lower ratios of capital to labor. While R&D expenditures are not significantly higher in firms with new product development except among the medium-sized ones, it is firms with a lower ratio of R&D personnel to total number of employees and a lower likelihood of having internationally certified products (such as ISO1990) that have a better chance of developing new products in the presence of FDI.

In other words, the firms reporting "innovations" are of the opposite type to the usual idea of current leading firms or high-tech and sophisticated firms being the innovators. Furthermore, in the presence of FDI, it is the firms with less foreign contact that are more likely to report new product development. In particular, the positive correlation between FDI presence and the likelihood of new product development is only observed among firms that do not use imported machinery or parts supplied by foreign firms, or produce final products, parts, or inputs for foreign firms — either of their own designs or to the specifications of foreign firms. Although counterintuitive at first glance, these findings are consistent with a story where increased incentives for *imitation* rather than true *innovation* are the main effects of FDI presence on Chinese domestic firms' innovation behaviors, the target market of these imitation products being the domestic market. As foreign firms mostly adopt mature technologies (see Chapter 2), the cost of imitation is reduced, making it easier to modify existing products with the aim of targeting the domestic market rather than developing authentically new products.

Our findings thus paint a picture that is far from simple regarding the net effects of FDI on Chinese firms. In each of the aspects that we have studied, there are both winners and losers due to the presence of foreign direct investment. To summarize, between target firms and domestic firms, firms targeted by foreign investment benefit more from FDI presence: Compared to domestic firms, foreign firms have higher TFP, pay higher wages, and export more, although they do not necessarily innovate more. Between skilled labor and unskilled workers, FDI presence drives up the wages of engineers and managers, but does not significantly impact the wage rate of production workers, at least up to the year 2000. Between private firms and SOEs, private firms experience substantially larger from the presence of FDI in China in productivity and employee wage and quality. Private firms do suffer a larger negative impact on export performance due to competition from foreign firms, which, however, may also indicate greater involvement in the global supply chain. Furthermore, between authentic innovators and imitators, it is the latter that benefits more from the presence of foreign-invested firms. Finally, there are also substantial variations in FDI effects across industries. In general, industries that compete less or less directly with foreign firms tend to benefit more. For example, there are more positive vertical spillovers than horizontal spillovers in TFP. Sectors suffering less negative FDI spillovers on exports are those in which foreign-invested firms themselves do not increase their foreign sales.

The mixed picture outlined above seems to defy the conventional wisdom that FDI has brought China unambiguously beneficial effects. Yet at the same time, we do observe that the large inflow of foreign capital into China has been accompanied by the breathtaking growth in the Chinese economy, and in addition, regions attracting more FDI also have registered more economic growth. As a result, our findings further beg the question of how exactly FDI relates to a region and a country's economic growth. While a careful study of this question requires another book-length project, we think the results from the current study suggest several specific directions for future research.

First of all, despite the sometimes ambiguous effects of foreign direct investment on domestic firms, one overall trend has developed along with FDI inflow, i.e., the greater involvement of Chinese firms in the economic globalization process. While firms with foreign investment increase their direct sales overseas, domestic firms are probably more engaged in supplying products to foreign-invested firms in China. The positive spillovers of FDI on TFP and wages of domestic firms also highlight the greater interactions between foreign capital and domestic entities. Future research could potentially explore the role of FDI in bringing about greater globalization and thus in influencing China's economic development.

Secondly, as most findings are specific to the ownership type of the firms, to the origin of the foreign capital, or to the industry, they suggest that it may be futile to explore the overall effects of FDI presence, especially in a country as large as China. Instead, a more fruitful way is to study the FDI effects at a disaggregated level, paying attention to many of the specific characteristics of the industry, the region, and the firms being studied. The detailed research focus again highlights the importance of more disaggregated data sets. Firm-level data thus should become indispensible for any studies of FDI effects.

In addition, our findings also suggest that the effects of foreign investment on firm performance and regional development depend on multiple factors, many of which may be institutional rather than technological in nature. In other words, to understand what conditions help promote positive FDI spillovers, we should pay more attention to the institutional features of both domestic firms, foreign investment, as well as their operating environments. And such institutional features should include ownership, investment contracting arrangements, and other firm-level characteristics, as well as industry competition, entry barriers, local business environment, government regulations, and other local information.

Finally, the effects that FDI may have on the host country should not be limited only to the firm level or only to the domain defined by technological improvements. In addition to affecting the FDI spillovers through facilitating or impeding the channels of technological and managerial expertise transfers, institutional factors also offer an important area where FDI presence can exert direct influence. Specifically, there are three broad categories of institutions that the presence of FDI may have helped improve. Given the greater reliance of foreign-invested firms on the formal legal system, the inflow of FDI may have helped speed up legal development in China. Similarly, the general expectations of foreign-invested firms to seek services and assistance from various government agencies and the government agencies' subsequent willingness to help may have spilled over to the government's attitudes toward domestic firms. Additionally, the inflow of FDI may have helped provide more equal access to finances for many domestic firms and in the process has improved the efficiency of the overall financial institutions in China.

Therefore, a big piece of the FDI story may still be missing without studying these other effects of FDI on the Chinese economy. For at least two reasons, these effects may not be captured in higher TFP at the firm level in a time-span of less than ten years, which is the time frame of most studies on FDI spillovers on TFP. First of all, if these institutions (legal, governance, and financial) improve in response to FDI presence, the beneficial impact will be on the whole economy where more new firms will emerge, which do not necessarily become the most productive and most efficient ones right away. Instead, the entry of a large number of new firms may initially be reflected in a lower average TFP to begin with, as firms do not have to enjoy a productivity (or profitability) "premium" in order to overcome the additional entry barriers imposed by inferior institutions. Secondly, the increased competition among a larger number of domestic firms as well as that between domestic and foreign-invested firms may help increase the long-run productivity of all Chinese firms. However, the firm-level analysis will miss the average improvement in all firms' performance because firms are benchmarked by other Chinese firms in these studies. Thus it is possible that all Chinese firms have improved their productivity level in the presence of FDI, yet this general improvement is not easy to measure, as it is included into the benchmark value used for comparison purposes.

Out of the several lines of research outlined above, the last two relate to the importance of institutions in studying FDI effects in the host country. In particular, institutional features play two separate yet related roles in evaluating the effects of FDI. Institutional quality at the regional and industry levels may help determine the specific effects of FDI on impacted firms. And many of these institutional features themselves may be transformed through the influence of FDI presence.

The focus on institutions is shared by Yasheng Huang in *Selling China*, in which he argues that the large FDI inflow to China, rather than reflecting the nation's great growth potential that attracts foreign capital, really indicates the various institutional weaknesses in China. These institutional weaknesses hamper the healthy development of Chinese domestic private firms and thus open up the opportunity for foreign investment. In this and other works, Huang goes on to argue that the large inflow of FDI into China further deprives Chinese domestic firms of growth opportunities, and thus helps explain China's lack of worldly renowned private firms and helps predict faster growth in India versus China in the near future.

As alluded to above, however, the findings made in the current book suggest that Huang's argument can be turned on its head. We believe that Huang made an insightful finding in linking the foreign-invested firms' advantaged status in China to the country's weak property right protection for its own private firms and their inferior access to finances and other resources. Yet the emergence and continued presence of these foreign-invested firms, in our minds, may have in turn helped improve the institutional environment faced by Chinese domestic private firms (of course together with other forces during the reform era). Our finding of private firms benefitting more from FDI presence may be explained by these firms' greater vitality. It is, however, also consistent with the argument of institutional improvements induced by foreign investment. And in any case, the large FDI inflow in China has been accompanied by strengthening of the private sector over time, suggesting that the presence of FDI may have been more conducive to the growth of Chinese private firms than previously thought.

The overall role of FDI, as a result, may well be a positive one for China's economic growth, particularly due to its beneficial impact on the country's institutions. And specifically, we suggest at least three aspects of China's institutional environment that have improved at the same time of the continued growth of FDI: the legal system, the government services, and the financial intermediation for Chinese domestic firms. But it will require future research to firmly establish such links.

Chapter 8

Technical Information

Here we describe the data sets that we used throughout the book in more detail, provide some useful summary statistics, and present the details of empirical methodology used in the preceding chapters.[*]

8.1. Data Sources

8.1.1. Manufacturing census data

Our firm-level data come from the Chinese Industrial Surveys of Medium-Sized and Large Firms for 2000–2006. Commonly referred to as the National Bureau of Statistics (NBS) manufacturing census, this data set includes all state-owned companies and private firms that are above certain size thresholds. The full data set consists of about 1.5 million observations (0.5 million firms) and is an unbalanced panel with a lot more firms coming into the sample in 2004 (a census year). Unfortunately, we are forced to drop many observations due to missing values for crucial variables, such as county or industry code; duplication (exact or approximate); negative values of assets or equity. For the purposes of our analysis we also have to drop from our sample firms that switch provinces during our sample period, because most of our analysis is on spillovers within province–industry cells. We end up with a sample of 267,990 firms. Our regression analysis, however, includes even fewer firms because, depending on specification, some observations drop out due to missing variables and their lags. Table 8.1 gives summary statistics by industry in 2006 for the final sample of firms that enter regressions.

Table 8.2 presents the composition of firms by ownership in our final sample for each of the years. We can see that the proportion of foreign-invested firms remained relatively stable throughout our sample period, while the share of foreign ownership, both from the Greater China Area and from other countries about doubled between 2000 and 2006, indicating

---

[*]This chapter is coauthored with Hirotaka Miura.

Table 8.1   Total number of employees, assets, and revenues in 2006 by sector.

| | Total | | | Average | | | | |
Sector	Employees	Assets	Revenues	FRN share	HMT share	Nominal wage	Foreign sales share	Number of firms
Textiles	5.611	1080.781	1370.789	0.065	0.116	13.273	0.238	23282
Electronics	4.318	1839.874	3016.323	0.420	0.272	25.925	0.592	8149
Mineral Prods.	3.974	1112.769	1050.787	0.047	0.051	13.988	0.121	20347
Apparel	3.437	340.972	517.741	0.165	0.263	14.789	0.524	12089
Electric Eq.	3.338	1133.991	1524.689	0.160	0.169	19.019	0.343	14542
Transport	3.272	1779.471	1797.338	0.122	0.044	23.040	0.139	11083
Equipment	3.094	968.329	1086.599	0.091	0.047	18.512	0.152	19628
Raw Chemicals	3.087	1591.312	1726.785	0.058	0.043	20.437	0.092	18488
Ferr. Smelting	2.710	2172.788	2395.099	0.027	0.033	26.421	0.067	5965
Agroproducts	2.214	638.175	1190.111	0.107	0.053	13.638	0.149	15345
Leather/Fur	2.080	196.282	353.115	0.210	0.297	14.440	0.586	6195
Metal Prods.	2.002	458.547	659.787	0.121	0.134	16.886	0.312	13157
Autos	1.897	1191.926	1303.794	0.161	0.040	23.548	0.105	7231
Spec. Equipment	1.880	619.492	631.104	0.093	0.070	19.923	0.118	9599
Paper	1.228	504.674	462.125	0.082	0.098	15.255	0.085	7266
Pharmaceutical	1.172	558.940	418.032	0.089	0.042	19.752	0.093	4875
Handicraft	1.104	123.287	201.031	0.148	0.246	14.271	0.596	4937
Food	1.103	317.094	393.095	0.154	0.080	15.528	0.116	5204
Nonferr. Smelt.	1.059	662.719	1043.329	0.039	0.037	21.485	0.093	4777
Sports Goods	1.006	99.862	147.947	0.197	0.421	15.604	0.694	3211
Computers	0.997	469.409	1139.631	0.604	0.271	26.712	0.739	968
Cons. Plastics	0.900	175.044	213.714	0.191	0.270	16.750	0.416	5857
Beverage	0.886	390.575	375.277	0.119	0.061	17.658	0.031	3683
Timber	0.812	139.691	209.537	0.066	0.069	12.865	0.191	5910
Ind. Plastics	0.742	249.515	305.441	0.097	0.116	15.404	0.145	5932
Instruments	0.737	192.552	263.219	0.265	0.224	22.069	0.467	3174
Furniture	0.735	113.438	153.060	0.182	0.263	16.326	0.518	3206
Western Meds.	0.712	359.939	279.136	0.108	0.042	21.522	0.122	2780
Rubber Prods.	0.658	199.226	234.867	0.156	0.121	15.909	0.260	2773
Printing	0.610	170.774	140.763	0.050	0.165	17.856	0.134	4534
Fuel Processing	0.550	527.953	1021.169	0.028	0.019	23.066	0.025	1893
Telecom	0.549	407.379	690.531	0.417	0.157	41.982	0.461	1013
Nonferr. Metals	0.423	138.746	162.285	0.010	0.005	18.043	0.023	1715
Ferrous Metals	0.412	129.280	128.105	0.002	0.002	18.384	0.002	2361
Nonmetals	0.403	76.801	86.271	0.010	0.011	14.313	0.034	2352
Chinese Meds.	0.398	186.246	124.229	0.048	0.040	17.343	0.026	1745
Chemical Fiber	0.337	211.390	229.748	0.052	0.078	17.019	0.072	1106
Overall Total	64.457	25859.898	27460.809	0.112	0.112	19.401	0.227	267990

Total number of employees is reported in millions of employees. Total assets and revenues are reported in millions of yuan. Averages are weighted by number of employees. HMT share is defined as Hong Kong–Macao–Taiwan capital as share of total paid-up capital. FRN share is defined as other foreign capital as share of total paid-up capital. Nominal wage equals total accrued payroll divided by number of employees and is reported in thousands of yuan per employee. Foreign sales share equals revenue from exports divided by total operation revenue.

Table 8.2 Composition of firms in final sample.

Year	2000	2001	2002	2003	2004	2005	2006
Total number of firms	134710	139167	147438	159754	240882	236786	267990
Fully domestic firms	111228	113634	120153	129594	193427	190317	217130
— Percent of total (%)	83	82	81	81	80	80	81
Firms with foreign share	23482	25533	27285	30160	47455	46469	50860
— Percent of total (%)	17	18	19	19	20	20	19
Firms with HMT share	12818	13926	14112	15666	24872	22613	24405
— Percent of total (%)	10	10	10	10	10	10	9
Firms with other foreign share	10252	11155	12703	14069	22107	23426	25986
— Percent of total (%)	8	8	9	9	9	10	10
Firms with major foreign share	13680	15857	17513	20320	33884	34065	37983
— Percent of total (%)	10	11	12	13	14	14	14
Firms with major HMT share	7546	8801	9248	10894	18398	17058	18720
— Percent of total (%)	6	6	6	7	8	7	7
Firms with major other foreign share	6065	6985	8195	9370	15403	16929	19177
— Percent of total (%)	5	5	6	6	6	7	7
Average foreign share (%)	10.54	12.51	13.59	15.91	19.86	21.15	22.42
Average HMT share (%)	5.79	6.82	7.3	8.63	10.98	10.63	11.19
Average other foreign share (%)	4.75	5.69	6.29	7.27	8.89	10.52	11.22

that foreign investors increased their stakes in the existing targets but did not invest much into new firms.

In studying direct effects of FDI, we use two samples: all firms, and firms that had positive shares of capital invested by firms from any foreign country, including HMT. We do this in order to isolate the effects of new foreign investment to firms that previously were 100% domestically-owned from those due to increase in foreign investment in firms that had previous foreign share. Since the majority of firms in our sample are fully domestic, as Table 8.2 shows, results from the full sample regressions are predominantly driven by new investment into previously domestic firms, while the results of regressions limited to firms with positive foreign shares are driven by increased foreign ownership. Note that cross-section differences between firms with and without foreign investment do not play a role, because they are absorbed by firm fixed effects in our regressions.

In studying spillovers, we exclude from the sample both HMT-invested firms and firms with investment from other foreign sources in any of the years in our sample. To explore the effects of domestic firms' own ownership type on FDI spillovers, we single out two ownership types: private firms (defined as firms with majority private share) and state-owned enterprises (SOEs) (defined as firms with majority state share). While these two groups do not span all firms in our sample due to complicated ownership structures in China, they represent "extreme" categories in the sense of the degree of governmental control. Firms that do not fit into these categories are about as numerous as private firms and enter our full sample regressions.

To construct capital input variable, we use the perpetual inventory method by applying the following procedure to each firm in the data set. Let K^o denote total fixed capital (original value). Let K^d denote nominal capital depreciated at 9% annual depreciation rate. Let subscript t denote time in year and let g_{it} denote the average of the year-on-year change in original value of fixed asset (reported by CEIC China Premium Database) in industry i over the years from $t-4$ to year t (We use the total original value of fixed assets of all firms in our sample if industry-level data are unavailable). Let b denote the birth year of the firm. If a firm first enters the data set at time s, the birth year initial total-fixed capital (original value) for the firm, K_0^o, is set equal to $K_s^o/((1+g_{i,s})^{(s-b)})$. Values for years between 0 and s are obtained by multiplying $1+g_{i,s}$ with the previous year's total-fixed capital (original value). Depreciated nominal capital stock at time t is calculated as $K_t^d = 0.91K_{t-1}^o + (K_t^o - K_{t-1}^o)$. Real capital stock is then obtained by deflating K_t^d using Chinese national headline CPI.

In our analysis we rely on the following variables:

Output: Total operation revenue in year 2000 RMB, used in logs.

Intermediate inputs: Throughput in year 2000 RMB, used in logs.

Capital input: Constructed using the perpetual inventory method with 9% annual depreciation rate, in year 2000 RMB as described above, used in logs.

Labor input: Number of employees, used in logs.

Firm age: Observation year less founding year of the firm. Observations with negative age and age greater than 52 are dropped.

Exports/sales: Export divided by total sales. Observations with negative values and values greater than or equal to 1.1 are dropped. Values greater than one and less than 1.1 are set to one.

New product/sales: New product output divided by total output. Cases where new product output is greater than total are replaced with missing. We also use an indicator of new product output being positive as an alternative measure for new product innovation.

Real wage: Total accrued payroll in year 2000 RMB divided by the number of employees, used in logs.

Leverage: Total debt divided by total assets. Negative leverage is replaced with zero.

State share: State shares divided by paid-up capital, restricted to [0, 1] interval.

FRN share: Foreign shares divided by paid-up capital, restricted to [0, 1] interval.

HMT share: Hong Kong, Macao, Taiwan shares divided by paid-up capital, restricted to [0, 1] interval.

8.1.2. World Bank 2001 and 2003 Investment Climate Surveys

When analysis requires information beyond that available in the balance sheets of the firms, we use data from the Study of Competitiveness, Technology and Firm Linkages conducted by the World Bank in 2001 and 2003. Each survey consists of two questionnaires, one filled out by the senior manager of the firm's main production facility, and the other filled out by the accountant and/or the personnel manager of the firm. The surveys collect detailed information on firms and their operation environment, and in 2001 the survey also includes more comprehensive questions regarding firms' labor force. Both surveys use stratified random sampling with stratification based on various subsectors covering both services and manufacturing. In 2001, a stratified random sample of 300 establishments is drawn from each of five cities in China: Beijing, Chengdu, Guangzhou, Shanghai, and Tianjin, giving a total sample size of 1500; while the 2003 survey included 2400 firms from 18 other cities.

Firms were interviewed only once, and for most of the variables, the firms were requested to provide information for the year prior to the survey year. However, for many accounting measures, information from up to three previous years was also collected. Firms in the first survey were interviewed in 2001 and provided information for the years 1998–2000, while firms in the second survey were interviewed in 2003 and their data correspond to 2000–2002. Thus in practice, each survey is a retrospective panel for these accounting measures.

In this study, we construct two samples based on the two surveys. The first sample is constructed from the 2001 survey to explore the labor market effects of FDI presence, thus we use a small portion of the data that give accounting information on firms' input (including wages and the

Table 8.3 Distribution of foreign and domestic firms in 2001 World Bank survey.

	All	Foreign	Domestic	Private share[a]
Number of firms	1500	382	1118	1118
By city:				
1. Beijing	300	75	225	0.31
2. Chengdu	300	32	268	0.39
3. Guangzhou	300	84	216	0.46
4. Shanghai	300	122	178	0.16
5. Tianjin	300	69	231	0.39
By industry:				
1. Accounting etc.	104	11	93	0.41
2. Advertising and marketing	89	15	74	0.39
3. Apparel and leather	222	63	159	0.36
4. Business logistics services	110	22	88	0.14
5. Communication services	71	3	68	0.12
6. Consumer products	165	40	125	0.39
7. Electronic components	203	77	126	0.36
8. Electronic equipment	192	65	127	0.37
9. IT services	128	21	107	0.49
10. Vehicles and parts	216	65	151	0.37

[a]For domestic firms only.

composition of the labor force), output, and ownership structure. Table 8.3 gives the city and sector distribution of firms included in the 2001 survey, which make up our first sample.[1] Among the 1500 firms interviewed during the survey, 382 were foreign firms in 2000.

The second sample is a combination of the two surveys with a research focus on firms' innovation, which implies that the combined sample only includes manufacturing firms. Table 8.4 gives the city and sector distribution of firms included in our second World Bank survey sample. Of the total number of 3900 surveyed firms, 2474 correspond to 47 four-digit level industries in the manufacturing sector, while the remaining 1426 firms correspond to services. The 47 manufacturing industries can be categorized in seven different groups: Apparel and Leather Goods, Household Appliances, Electronic Equipment, Electronic Components, Vehicles and Vehicle Parts, Metallurgical Products, Food Processing, and Chemical, Bio-tech and Medicine.[2] We work with private domestic firms in the manufacturing sector, which account for 1055 firms. For the second sample, we use data on inputs, output, exports, introduction of new goods, expenditure in R&D, suppliers, competitors, market environment, ownership structure, characteristics of the labor force, use of technology, and interactions with foreign firms located in China.

[1]For a detailed description of the survey, see Hallward-Driemeier, Wallsten, and Xu (2003).
[2]Some of the 47 industries were not included in the first survey.

Table 8.4 Distribution of manufacturing firms in 2001 and 2003 World Bank surveys.

	All	Domestic	Private domestic
Number of firms	2563	2036	1055

By city:

Beijing	198	151	61
Chengdu	200	179	86
Guangzhou	200	130	87
Shanghai	200	100	51
Tianjin	200	147	70
Benxi	62	57	25
Changchun	100	71	34
Changsha	100	91	45
Chongqing	100	75	45
Dalian	67	50	32
Guiyang	100	94	42
Haerbin	100	93	28
Hangzhou	67	42	30
Jiangmen	66	46	32
Kunming	100	95	39
Lanzhou	99	97	29
Nanchang	98	88	43
Nanning	73	67	30
Shenzhen	67	40	28
Wenzhou	66	59	56
Wuhan	100	79	47
Xian	100	93	45
Zhengzhou	100	92	70

By industry:

Sector	Total	Domestic	Private
Apparel and leather	575	457	253
Electronic equipment	377	277	175
Electronic components	479	367	178
Appliances	228	172	91
Vehicles and parts	574	456	220
Food	71	62	37
Chemical and medicine	66	62	26
Biotech and Chinese med.	36	34	25
Metallurgical products	157	147	50

Specifically, we use the following variables directly or constructed from the survey, with all values referring to year 2000 unless indicated otherwise:

Value added: Firm sales (adjusted by change in final product inventory) minus total material costs, in year 2000 RMB, used in logs.

Employment: Number of employees in the firm.

Nonproduction workers: Percentage of employees involved in management or engineering.

Capital input: Value of fixed assets in year 2000 RMB, used in logs.

Labor input: Number of employees in the firm, used in logs.

Capital/Labor: Capital intensity of the firm, measured as the ratio between capital input and labor input.

Firm age: Firm's age.

Average education: Average education level of production workers, engineering, and managerial personnel in the firm, in years of schooling.

Average age: Average age of production workers, engineering, and managerial personnel in the firm, in years.

Average foreign experience: Average foreign experience of engineering and managerial personnel in the firm, in years.

Market share: Firm's self-reported market share in main line of operation.

Exporter: An indicator for whether the firm is exporting some of its products.

Transportation cost: Transportation expenses divided by sales.

Industry: Industry sector of the firm, a categorical variable $1, 2, \ldots, 10$.

City: City where the firm is located, a categorical variable $1, 2, \ldots, 5$.

Largest foreign partner: The share of the largest foreign partner in firm's ownership in 1999.

Private ownership share: Total share of private ownership, including portfolio investment in 1999.

Foreign ownership share: Total share of foreign ownership, including portfolio investment in 1999.

Share of foreign sales: Foreign sales divided by total sales in 1999.

Imported machinery: Dummy variable indicating whether the firm has imported machinery in the previous year.

Used parts supplied by foreign firms: Dummy variable indicating whether the firm has used parts supplied by foreign firms in the previous year.

Produced final products for foreign firms: Dummy variable indicating whether the firm produced final products for foreign firms in the previous year.

Produced parts or inputs for foreign firms: Dummy variable indicating whether the firm has produced parts or inputs for foreign firms in the previous year.

Produced to the specifications of foreign firms: Dummy variable indicating whether the firm has produced products to the specifications of foreign firms in the previous year.

Produced for foreign firms of its own design: Dummy variable indicating whether the firm has produced for foreign firms of its own design in the previous year.

I(Patent): An indicator of whether the firm owned a patent.

Number of patent applications: Number of patent applications filed.

I(New products): An indicator of whether the firm developed new products.

R&D/Sales: Ratio of R&D expenditures to sales.

R&D employment: Percentage of employees involved in R&D.

Certified products (ISO 9000): Indicator for whether the firm has certified products (by ISO 9000, etc.).

8.2. Empirical Approach

8.2.1. Measures of FDI presence

8.2.1.1. NBS manufacturing census data

To measure the presence of FDI, we construct the weighted average foreign share of all firms located in the same province and in the same two-digit China Industry Code (CIC) sector, with each firm's employment as the weight. To distinguish the potentially different effects of investment from different foreign origins, we compute the FDI presence measure separately for investment from Hong Kong–Macao–Taiwan (HMT) and that from other foreign sources (FRN).

To study vertical FDI spillovers, we use China's Input–Output Table of 2002 (122 sectors) to compute the *upstream* FDI presence and *downstream* FDI presence for each industry i. Based on the within industry FDI presence of all other two-digit CIC industries that serve as suppliers to industry i, as computed above, we construct the *upstream* FDI for industry i. In particular, it is the sum of FDI presence in all these industries (excluding the industry to which firm i belongs) in the same province weighted by the *input* coefficients of these industries corresponding to firm i's industry. The *downstream* FDI presence, on the other hand, is computed as the sum of FDI presence in all the client industries of i, weighted by the *output* coefficients of industry i to these other industries.

Specifically, we construct the complete output coefficient matrix (containing a coefficient for each pair of industries), $\mathbf{B}$, as

$$\mathbf{B} = (\mathbf{I} - \mathbf{A})^{-1} - \mathbf{I},$$

where $\mathbf{I}$ is the identity matrix and $\mathbf{A}$ is the direct output coefficient matrix, which is in turn computed by dividing the direct usage of the output of industry i in industry j, by the total output of industry i. In other words, industry i's output will impact industry j both directly by being used in j as input, and indirectly by being used as inputs in other industries, which in turn produce outputs that are used as inputs in industry j.

In computing the direct and complete coefficients, we include the impact of imported goods in each industry, but exclude the impact of export goods. This is a different approach than used by Girma and Görg (2007), who exclude imported inputs. We believe that including imported inputs is important because they might be one of the channels by which foreign firms bring in new technology into China. Finally, we compute for each industry i a weighted average of the FDI presence in all other industries that serve as its clients with the complete *output* coefficient as the weight. This measure is referred to as the forward linkage (or downstream FDI presence). The backward linkage measure is computed similarly, except with complete *input* coefficient matrix.

8.2.1.2. *World Bank survey data*

Based on the information on firms' foreign ownership, we construct the measure of FDI presence as follows: For each domestic firm, we identify the city–sector cell where the firm is located. We then compute the weighted

Table 8.5   FDI presence by city and industry sector in 1999.

Sector, city	Beijing	Chengdu	Guangzhou	Shanghai	Tianjin	Overall
Accounting and related services	0.186	0.000	0.011	0.000	0.022	0.048
Advertising and marketing	0.036	0.008	0.013	0.095	0.193	0.074
Apparel and leather goods	0.162	0.009	0.212	0.174	0.311	0.172
Business logistics services	0.006	0.000	0.032	0.040	0.044	0.024
Communication services	0.000	0.008	0.000	0.000	0.008	0.003
Consumer products	0.097	0.061	0.108	0.185	0.324	0.161
Electronic components	0.149	0.038	0.207	0.302	0.458	0.231
Electronic equipment	0.253	0.014	0.065	0.353	0.240	0.189
Information technology services	0.052	0.068	0.020	0.154	0.009	0.054
Vehicles and vehicle parts	0.123	0.096	0.125	0.238	0.121	0.139
Overall	0.129	0.036	0.104	0.186	0.209	0.133

average of the largest foreign partner's share in each firm located in the same city–sector, as of 1999, with firm employment as the weight.[3] The average foreign share thus obtained is referred to as the "FDI presence" in the city–sector cell. Our focus, therefore, is the effect of FDI presence within the same geographic location and industry. Table 8.5 gives the average foreign share by city and industry sector based on the 2001 World Bank survey data.

It is clear from Table 8.5 that there is substantially greater FDI presence in manufacturing sectors than in service sectors, which is consistent with the Chinese policies toward FDI. Compared to FDI measures based on the NBS manufacturing census data (see Table 1.1), however, the World Bank survey sample gives higher average level of FDI in manufacturing sectors. And the percentage of manufacturing firms with foreign shares is also higher in the World Bank surveys than that in the NBS manufacturing census (compare Tables 1.2 and 1.3 with Tables 8.3 and 8.4). This is due to the fact that only major cities are included in the survey, which tend to have greater FDI presence. In other words, the World Bank survey data

---

[3]The only exception is in the chapter studying the innovation effects of FDI presence, where firm sales is used as the weight.

may not be representative of the whole nation. As a result, we use FDI measures computed from the NBS census data as alternative measures in some specifications.

8.2.2. Productivity measures

We define total factor productivity (TFP) as the residuals generated from estimating a dynamic production function of the form:

$$y_{it} = \alpha_0 + \alpha_1 y_{i,t-1} + \alpha_2 l_{it} + \alpha_3 k_{it} + \alpha_4 m_{it} + \eta_i + v_{it}$$
$$\mathrm{E}[\eta_i] = \mathrm{E}[v_{it}] = \mathrm{E}[\eta_i v_{it}] = 0 \tag{8.1}$$

where y_{it} is log of output by firm i at time t, k_{it} is log of capital, l_{it} is log of employment, m_{it} is log of intermediate inputs, whereas η_i is the firm-specific fixed effect, and v_{it} is a random error term. Output, capital, and intermediate inputs are all deflated to 2000 prices using Chinese national headline CPI. Capital stock is generated by implementing the perpetual inventory method as in Brandt, Van Biesebroeck, and Zhang (2009).

In designing the estimation approach, the following characteristics of our data need to be taken into account. First, there is high autocorrelation in both left- and right-hand side variables. Second, explanatory variables may be endogenously determined. Third, our panel is wide (large N) and short (small T). Moreover, firm fixed effects need to be included to account for unobserved time-invariant differences across firms. Though a variety of methods exist that can be implemented to estimate Eq. (8.1), data limitations constrain our choice of estimators. Ordinary least squares (OLS) and fixed effect (FE) estimators are not optimal in accommodating the first and the third data features above.[4] We also encounter several estimation issues when implementing the Levinsohn and Petrin (2003) method, which include lack of convergence in some industries and a persistent TFP measure. The Olley and Pakes (1996) method, which requires information on firm exits, would further limit our sample since we do not have data on firm exits for the last year of our sample. Thus, in order to estimate (8.1) and obtain reasonable residuals we have to rely on "internal" instruments that are based on lags of the instrumented variables using the system generalized method of moments (GMM) estimator developed by Arellano and Bover (1995) and Blundell and Bond (1998).

System GMM combines equations in the first differences and in the levels. The former eliminates firm-specific fixed effects and uses the lagged

---

[4]The asymptotic properties of OLS and FE estimators can be modified to take into account the inclusion of the lagged dependent variable on the right-hand side (Greene, 2008, Section 4.9.6), however, the consistency of the estimators depend on $T \to \infty$ (Greene, 2008, Section 15.6.5).

levels of variables as valid instruments. The latter exploits additional moment conditions in the levels equations that enable the use of lagged differences of variables as valid instruments. The equations in levels address the problem of finite sample bias, which arises from the lagged levels of the variables providing weak instruments for first-differences (see Alonso-Borrego and Arellano, 1999). Exogeneity of instruments are tested using the Arellano–Bond (1991) test for autocorrelation.[5]

In conforming with established practices, we use the lags of levels and first-differences of covariates $y_{i,t-1}$, l_{it}, k_{it}, and m_{it} as GMM style instruments. We account for the endogeneity of $y_{i,t-1}$ by using instruments lagged $t - 3$ and earlier for equations in first-differences and $\Delta y_{i,t-2}$ for the levels equations. This is done to avoid the violation of moment conditions $E[y_{i,t-2}\Delta v_{it}] = 0$ and $E[\Delta y_{i,t-1}v_{it}] = 0$. For the other three covariates l_{it}, k_{it}, and m_{it}, all possible lags in levels are used as instruments in the first-differenced equations and first-differences Δl_{it}, Δk_{it}, and Δm_{it} are used in the levels equations. We estimate production functions for each industry based on two-step system GMM with robust standard errors, thus allowing production functions to vary across industries.[6] There should be minimal first-order autocorrelation of v_{it} and the moment conditions pertaining to our specified instruments should hold, thus we expect to not reject the Arellano–Bond test for AR(2). We also do not expect to reject the Wald test of constant returns to scale hypothesis: $\alpha_2 + \alpha_3 + \alpha_4 = 1$.

Estimation results, reported in Table 8.6, for the sample of domestic firms are fairly consistent with our expectations. For all industries, we fail to reject the Arellano–Bond test for AR(2) at 13% or lower significance level. Autocorrelation of the random error term in the levels equations has been removed and our specified instruments are valid. Only for a few industries can we reject constant returns to scale at the 5% level, which suggest potentially inefficient scale of production in sectors such as Agroproducts, Food, Beverage, Fuel Processing, Mineral Products, Ferrous Smelting, Equipment, Electric Equipment, and Electronics. Finally, for each firm, TFP is set equal to v_{it}. In a recent paper Brandt, Van Biesebroeck,

---

[5]The Arellano–Bond (1991) test for autocorrelation tests the null of zero pth-order autocorrelation in the first-differenced error term (Δv_{it}). In general, AR(p) in first-differences must be checked in order to assess AR($p - 1$) in levels, and thus the test statistic of main concern is AR(2). We do not report results of the Sargan (1958, 1959) test. The Sargan test of over-identifying restrictions, which tests the null that the instruments as a group are exogenous, is not robust to heteroskedasticity and autocorrelation and has been shown to over-reject in large samples with persistent series (Blundell and Bond (2000) and Blundell, Bond, and Windmeijer (2001)).

[6]Additional adjustments include the following: For Textile and Electric Equipment industries we drop outliers in the top and bottom 1%. In addition, we separate the Plastic Products industry into two subsectors: Industrial and Consumer Plastics.

Table 8.6 System GMM production function estimations.

Sector	Constant	Lagged output	Capital	Labor	Throughput	AR(2)	CRS	N	N-g	j
Ferrous Metals	-0.003 (0.161)	0.060*** (0.014)	0.072*** (0.025)	0.058** (0.024)	0.886*** (0.022)	0.316	0.537	4620	2110	93
Nonferr. Metals	-0.272 (0.181)	0.121*** (0.022)	-0.002 (0.022)	0.025 (0.029)	0.931*** (0.019)	0.723	0.223	4154	1740	93
Nonmetals	-0.620** (0.245)	0.138*** (0.021)	0.163*** (0.036)	0.089*** (0.029)	0.774*** (0.024)	0.425	0.530	6567	2727	93
Agroproducts	-0.584*** (0.081)	0.102*** (0.010)	0.121*** (0.012)	0.121*** (0.013)	0.825*** (0.013)	0.895	0.000	40298	16201	93
Food	-0.665*** (0.128)	0.118*** (0.016)	0.151*** (0.022)	0.126*** (0.021)	0.780*** (0.021)	0.437	0.018	13061	5074	93
Beverage	-1.580*** (0.284)	0.140*** (0.019)	0.194*** (0.041)	0.126*** (0.026)	0.807*** (0.021)	0.853	0.004	11056	4082	93
Textiles	-0.232*** (0.060)	0.059*** (0.005)	0.094*** (0.008)	0.038*** (0.008)	0.887*** (0.008)	0.160	0.060	51509	19766	93
Garments	0.104 (0.113)	0.092*** (0.012)	0.073*** (0.012)	0.118*** (0.015)	0.798*** (0.018)	0.535	0.528	19935	7829	93
Leather/Fur	0.033 (0.101)	0.088*** (0.014)	0.067*** (0.013)	0.113*** (0.019)	0.820*** (0.023)	0.927	0.994	10504	4277	93
Timber	-0.162 (0.116)	0.058*** (0.012)	0.090*** (0.023)	0.076*** (0.017)	0.871*** (0.022)	0.241	0.067	11581	5204	93
Furniture	0.329*** (0.120)	0.071*** (0.015)	0.051*** (0.017)	0.148*** (0.029)	0.804*** (0.029)	0.375	0.887	5408	2257	93
Paper	-0.274** (0.109)	0.106*** (0.011)	0.092*** (0.015)	0.092*** (0.019)	0.817*** (0.021)	0.318	0.945	20916	7512	93
Printing	-0.419*** (0.127)	0.158*** (0.023)	0.143*** (0.022)	0.150*** (0.024)	0.708*** (0.020)	0.251	0.964	15025	5135	93
Sports Goods	0.307* (0.187)	0.082*** (0.019)	0.078*** (0.019)	0.077*** (0.027)	0.806*** (0.034)	0.917	0.167	5011	2004	93
Fuel Processing	0.487*** (0.108)	0.048*** (0.011)	0.068*** (0.018)	0.023 (0.019)	0.860*** (0.018)	0.899	0.002	4806	1947	93
Raw Chemicals	-0.448*** (0.087)	0.098*** (0.009)	0.105*** (0.014)	0.082*** (0.015)	0.842*** (0.015)	0.320	0.091	46742	17172	93
Pharmaceutical	-0.422** (0.175)	0.168*** (0.017)	0.096*** (0.018)	0.114*** (0.030)	0.746*** (0.021)	0.138	0.189	13796	4697	93
Chemical Fiber	0.576** (0.258)	0.045*** (0.015)	-0.009 (0.018)	0.017 (0.031)	0.917*** (0.022)	0.604	0.068	2454	968	93
Rubber Prods.	-0.712*** (0.214)	0.106*** (0.024)	0.117*** (0.029)	0.109*** (0.034)	0.835*** (0.036)	0.558	0.100	6305	2364	93
Ind. Plastics	-0.292* (0.169)	0.107*** (0.017)	0.132*** (0.029)	0.086*** (0.025)	0.793*** (0.030)	0.477	0.707	13562	5589	93
Cons. Plastics	0.294** (0.128)	0.103*** (0.016)	0.041** (0.016)	0.137*** (0.024)	0.791*** (0.026)	0.402	0.124	8977	4011	93
Mineral Prods.	-0.846*** (0.100)	0.121*** (0.009)	0.119*** (0.013)	0.092*** (0.012)	0.836*** (0.012)	0.532	0.003	62785	22131	93
Ferr. Smelting	0.019 (0.075)	0.033*** (0.007)	0.056*** (0.017)	0.059*** (0.017)	0.912*** (0.018)	0.700	0.039	15626	6484	93
Nonferr. Smelt.	-0.164 (0.118)	0.045*** (0.011)	0.071*** (0.011)	0.017 (0.018)	0.927*** (0.017)	0.219	0.548	10483	4226	93
Metal Prods.	0.078 (0.109)	0.109*** (0.011)	0.110*** (0.011)	0.132*** (0.019)	0.752*** (0.024)	0.193	0.720	27922	11325	93
Equipment	-0.119** (0.059)	0.116*** (0.010)	0.069*** (0.010)	0.015 (0.011)	0.853*** (0.011)	0.424	0.000	44929	17022	93
Spec. Equipment	-0.298** (0.121)	0.123*** (0.016)	0.067*** (0.016)	0.026 (0.022)	0.861*** (0.017)	0.467	0.093	22258	8512	93
Transport	-0.087 (0.099)	0.100*** (0.016)	0.094*** (0.016)	0.084*** (0.019)	0.809*** (0.016)	0.749	0.586	28281	10258	93
Electric Eq.	-0.395*** (0.066)	0.083*** (0.008)	0.094*** (0.011)	0.091*** (0.011)	0.857*** (0.010)	0.242	0.002	31859	11823	93
Electronics	0.396** (0.180)	0.192*** (0.026)	-0.024 (0.029)	0.121*** (0.033)	0.753*** (0.031)	0.329	0.000	10388	4064	93
Instruments	0.157 (0.209)	0.159*** (0.042)	0.050* (0.030)	0.071** (0.034)	0.773*** (0.030)	0.389	0.061	6093	2348	93
Handicraft	0.091 (0.119)	0.081*** (0.017)	0.060*** (0.014)	0.081*** (0.017)	0.844*** (0.018)	0.743	0.417	9153	3726	93

Dependent variable is output. All variables in logs. Two-step system GMM estimation. Robust standard errors in parentheses. Firms with nonzero other foreign (FRN) share and Hong Kong–Macao–Taiwan (HMT) share excluded. AR(2) is the p-value of the Arellano–Bond test statistic which tests the null of zero 2nd-order autocorrelation in the first-differenced error term. CRS is the p-value from the Wald test of constant returns to scale hypothesis $\beta_k + \beta_l + \beta_m = 1$.

and Zhang (2009) provide a very careful estimation of TFP using the same data set as we do and various alternative methods, with fewer restrictions on the sample. Encouragingly, the descriptive statistics of our TFP measures are very close to theirs.

8.2.3. Estimating the effects of FDI presence

As discussed in Chapter 1, three potential biases need to be addressed in estimating the effects of FDI presence on various performance measures: the aggregation bias, the selection bias, and the standard error clustering bias. To properly address the aggregation bias, we rely on firm-level analysis and split foreign firms from domestic firms in our analysis. To handle the endogeneity bias, we will rely on fixed effects estimation whenever possible, as discussed below. Furthermore, we always cluster the standard errors at the same level of the FDI measure in our estimations. For example, when the FDI measure is constructed at the sector-province level, we cluster the standard errors at the same sector-province level in the corresponding estimations. Because of the different nature of our data sets, we have to use different measures and methods of analysis, which we now describe.

Census data analysis

For the analysis of direct effects of FDI on TFP, we augment model 8.1 with shares of capital paid up by investors from Hong Kong, Macao, Taiwan (HMT share) or from other foreign countries (FRN share) and estimated it using system GMM. For direct effects on other variables, we estimate models using firm fixed effects regression including relevant control variables as described in Chapter 2. More specifically, we estimate

$$Y_{ispt} = \alpha_i + \alpha_t + \beta_1 \mathrm{FRN}_{ispt-1} + \beta_2 \mathrm{HMT}_{ispt-1} + \mathbf{Z}'_{ispt}\Gamma + \varepsilon_{it}, \qquad (8.2)$$

where Y is a variable of interest for firm i in sector s province p and year t; α_i and α_t are firm and year-fixed effects; FRN and HMT are shares of foreign capital in firm i's capital; thus, coefficients β_1 and β_2 measure the effects of respective foreign shares on our outcome variables, conditional on firm heterogeneity, common time effects, as well as a vector of firm-level control variables, $\mathbf{Z}$.

Although the vector $\mathbf{Z}$ is empty for the estimation of FDI direct effects on TFP, the vector includes additional controls in other direct effect estimations. In particular, to estimate the direct effects of FDI on wages, we use average wage (total wage/number of employees) as the dependent variable, while $\mathbf{Z}$ includes the size of the firm (measured by log(employee)), capital intensity (the asset/employee ratio), as well as the share of capital paid up by state investors. For the direct effects of FDI on exports, the dependent variable is the firm's ratio between export and total sales, while **Z** includes firm size (log(employee)), firm age, and leverage (asset/liability). The estimation on how FDI presence affects innovation in target firms relies on the same specification as that for exports, except that the dependent variable is the dummy indicating whether the firm has positive new product sales. We also use the new product sales/total sales ratio as the dependent variable and achieve very similar results.

For the analysis of spillover effects on TFP and other variables of interest, we use the residual from regression 8.1 for TFP or another variable we want to analyze as the dependent variable, such as wage, foreign sales, or some innovation measure, and regress it on the average measure of FDI presence, limiting our sample to domestic firms only. Specifically, we estimate the following regression for horizontal spillovers

$$Y_{ispt} = \alpha_i + \alpha_t + \beta_1 \text{AFRN}_{spt-1} + \beta_2 \text{AHMT}_{spt-1} + \mathbf{Z}'_{ispt}\Gamma + \varepsilon_{it}, \quad (8.3)$$

where Y is again the variable of interest for firm i in sector s province p and year t; AFRN and AHMT are measures of average FDI presence in sector s province p lagged one year; and error term ε_{it} is allowed to be AR(1).

Similarly, for the analysis of vertical spillovers on TFP, we replace AFRN_{spt-1} and AHMT_{spt-1} with average shares of FDI presence in upstream and downstream industries as described above. We estimate these regressions for the full sample, and for private and SOE firms, separately. We also conduct the analysis by sector, again for all firms, and for private and SOE firms, separately. Coefficients β_1 and β_2 measure effects of foreign presence on our outcome variables conditional on firm heterogeneity, common time effects, and control variables.

While most of the results are reported at the two-digit CIC sector, there are a few three-digit sectors that we find particularly interesting. First of all, we consider it crucial to separate pharmaceutical industry into Chinese traditional medicines and western medicines, because there may not be much room for spillovers in traditional Chinese medicine sector. Next, within the electronics industry we study computer and telecommunication sectors, separately, mainly because we know that FDI into the computer industry occurred mostly prior to our sample period, while FDI into telecommunications occurred mostly during our sample period. We also isolate the auto industry from the overall transportation industry, because this is an industry that has drawn a lot of attention due to the large FDI inflow into China. Finally, we found it useful to split plastics into industrial and consumer plastics to estimate the production function and maintain the categorization below.

World Bank survey data analysis

For the analysis of the direct effects of foreign investment on labor quality and wages in target firms, we use the following specification:

$$Y_{isk} = \alpha_{sk} + \beta \text{FOR}_{isk} + \mathbf{Z}'_{isk}\Gamma + \varepsilon_{isk}, \tag{8.4}$$

where Y_{jik} is an outcome variable, such as average production worker education, age, or wage, in the firm i operating in sector s and city k, α_{ik} are city–industry fixed effects, FOR_{isk} is the share of foreign ownership in firm i that operates in industry s and city k, $\mathbf{Z}_{isk}$ is a set of firm-level control variables specific to the outcome variable, while ϵ_{isk} is a robust error term. The coefficient β on FOR_{isk} measures the direct effect of foreign direct investment on our outcome variables, conditional on city–industry heterogeneity and control variables.

To focus on the contrast between foreign and domestic firms, we exclude state-owned firms in this stage of the analysis. And the detailed information provided in the data allow us to study the wages for production workers, engineers, and managers, separately. For estimating the direct effects of foreign capital on wages, the control variables $\mathbf{Z}_{isk}$ include capital intensity (log (assets/employee)), as well as labor quality measures such as average age, average age squared, and average education of the relevant group (production workers, engineers, or managers). For wages of engineers and managers, we are also able to control for their average foreign experience. When studying the direct effects of foreign capital on labor quality, the control variables include firm age and firm size (measured in log (assets)).

When studying the spillover effects of FDI presence, we include both SOEs and domestic private firms. To first document differences between SOEs and private firms, we restrict our analysis to firms with no foreign partners and estimate the following specification:

$$Y_{isk} = \alpha_{sk} + \beta PR_{isk} + \mathbf{Z}'_{isk}\Gamma + \varepsilon_{isk}, \tag{8.5}$$

where PR_{isk} is the share of private ownership of the firm i and other variables are the same as defined above. The coefficient β on PR_{isk} measures the difference between SOEs and private firms.

Then to measure differential spillover effects of FDI on labor quality and wages of domestic private firms and SOEs, we use the following specification, again limiting our sample to the firms with zero foreign ownership:

$$Y_{isk} = \alpha_s + \alpha_k + \beta_1 \text{AFDI}_{sk} + \beta_2 PR_{isk}$$
$$+ \beta_3 \text{AFDI}_{sk} \cdot PR_{isk} + \mathbf{Z}'_{isk}\Gamma + \varepsilon_{isk}, \tag{8.6}$$

where AFDI_{sk} is a measure of average FDI presence in industry s and city k and α_s and α_k are sector and city-fixed effects, which we include separately because our measure of FDI presence does not vary within city–industry cell. The coefficient β_1 measures the effect of FDI presence on firms with zero private ownership, i.e., SOEs, while the sum $\beta_1 + \beta_3$ measure the effect of FDI presence on firms with 100% private ownership.

For the analysis of innovation and imitation we have more years of data and therefore, we can analyze the data conditioning on firm fixed effects. Specifically, we estimate variations of equations of the following general form over the sample of domestic firms

$$Y_{ist} = \alpha_i + \alpha_t \mathbf{Z}'_{ist} \gamma + \beta \text{FOR}_{st} + \varepsilon_{ist}, \qquad (8.7)$$

where i denotes firms, s industries, and t time. The dependent variable Y_{ist} is our variable of interest, for example, it indicates whether firm i in industry s introduced a new product variety during year t. And in some specifications, the dependent variable is the ratio between expenditure on R&D and firm sales. The variable FOR_{st} is defined as the share of foreign firms in total output in industry s in year t, and, thus, β measures the effect of foreign presence on the probability of introducing a new product. We cluster the standard errors at the industry-level.

In studying the innovation behaviors of firms, we restrict our sample to private firms that are 100% domestically-owned, because we are interested in the effect of foreign capital inflows on domestic firms and because state-owned enterprises may have different incentives to innovate (Cheung, 2007).

Note that we adopt the linear specification here that allows us to deal with unobserved heterogeneity. It could be argued that Eq. (8.7) can be modeled using nonlinear specifications such as probit in the case of introduction of new goods, and tobit in the case of expenditure on R&D. However, firm fixed effects cannot be differenced out in probit and tobit specifications and they create a problem of incidental parameters that invalidates estimates of all coefficients. It is in principle possible to difference out fixed effects using a conditional logit. This estimator, however, relies only on observations in which there is a "switch" in the dependent variable (from 0 to 1, or from 1 to 0). Given our relatively small sample size, it is very costly to lose the valuable information provided by "non-switchers" and the estimates obtained with this method are too imprecise.

Bibliography

Aghion, P, R Blundell, R Griffith, P Howitt and S Prantl (2009). The effects of entry on incumbent innovation and productivity. *Review of Economics and Statistics*, 91(1), 20–32.

Aitken, B and A Harrison (1999). Do domestic firms benefit from direct foreign investment? Evidence from Venezuela. *American Economic Review*, 89(3), 605–618.

Aitken, B, A Harrison and RE Lipsey (1996). Wages and foreign ownership: A comparative study of Mexico, Venezuela, and the United States. *Journal of International Economics*, 40(3–4), 345–371.

Akimova, I and G Schwödiauer (2004). Ownership structure, corporate governance, and enterprise performance: Empirical results for Ukraine. *International Advances in Economic Research*, 10(1), 28–42.

Alfaro, L and A Rodríguez-Clare (2004). Multinationals and linkages: An empirical investigation. *Economia*, 4(2), 113–169.

Almeida, R (2007). The labor market effects of foreign owned firms. *Journal of International Economics*, 72(1), 75–96.

Alonso-Borrego, C and M Arellano (1999). Symmetrically Normalized Instrumental-Variable Estimation Using Panel Data. *Journal of Business & Economic Statistics*, American Statistical Association, 17(1), 36–49, January.

Amiti, M and BS Javorcik (2008). Trade costs and location of foreign firms in China. *Journal of Development Economics*, 85, 129–149.

Arellano, M and S Bond (1991). Some tests of specification for panel data: Monte Carlo evidence and an application to employment equations. *Review of Economic Studies*, 58(2), 277–297.

Arellano, M and O Bover (1995). Another look at the instrumental variable estimation of error-components models. *Journal of Econometrics*, 68(1), 29–51.

Arnold, J and BS Javorcik (2009). Gifted kids or pushy parents? Foreign acquisitions and plant performance in Indonesia. *Journal of International Economics*, 79(1), 42–53.

Barrios, S, H Görg and E Strobl (2003). Explaining firms' export behaviour: R&D, spillovers and the destination market. *Oxford Bulletin of Economics and Statistics*, 65(4), 475–496.

Barry, F, H Görg and E Strobl (2005). Foreign direct investment and wages in domestic firms in Ireland: Productivity spillovers versus labour-market crowding out. *International Journal of the Economics of Business*, 12(1), 67–84.

Bartel, AP and AE Harrison (2005). Ownership versus environment: Disentangling the sources of public-sector inefficiency. *Review of Economics and Statistics*, 87(1), 135–147.

Blalock, G and P Gertler (2008). Welfare gains from foreign direct investment through technology transfer to local suppliers. *Journal of International Economics*, 74(2), 402–421.

Blomström, M and A Kokko (1998). Multinational corporations and spillovers. *Journal of Economic Surveys*, 12(2), 1–31.

Blonigen, BA and MJ Slaughter (2001). Foreign-affiliate activity and U.S. skill upgrading. *Review of Economics and Statistics*, 83(2), 362–376.

Blundell, R and S Bond (1998). Initial conditions and moment restrictions in dynamic panel data models. *Journal of Econometrics*, 87(1), 115–143.

Blundell, R and S Bond (2000). GMM estimation with persistent panel data: An application to production functions. *Econometric Reviews*, 19(3), 321–340.

Blundell, R, S Bond and F Windmeijer (2001). *Nonstationary Panels, Panel Cointegration, and Dynamic Panels*, Vol. 15 of *Advances in Econometrics*. JAI Press, Estimation in dynamic panel data models: Improving on the performance of the standard GMM estimators.

Braconier, H, P-J Norback and D Urban (2005). Multinational enterprises and wage costs: Vertical FDI revisited. *Journal of International Economics*, 67(2), 446–470.

Brambilla, I (2009). Multinationals, technology, and the introduction of varieties of goods. *Journal of International Economics*, 79(1), 89–101.

Brambilla, I, G Hale and C Long (2009). Foreign direct investment and the incentives to innovate and imitate. *Scandinavian Journal of Economics*, 111(4), 835–861.

Brandt, L, J Van Biesebroeck and Y Zhang (2009). Creative accounting or creative destruction? Firm-level productivity growth in Chinese manufacturing. *Journal of Development Economics*, forthcoming.

Candelaria, C, M Daly and G Hale (2009). Interprovincial inequality in China. *FRBSF Economic Letter*, 2009-13.

Chen, H and D Swenson (2009). Multinational exposure and the quality of new Chinese exports. Mimeo, available at http://www.econ.

ucdavis.edu/faculty/dswenson/ChinaExportQuality_September201%0.
pdf.

Cheng, LK and YK Kwan (2000). What are the determinants of the location of foreign direct investment? The Chinese experience. *Journal of International Economics*, 51, 379–400.

Cheung, K-Y (2007). The impact of ownership on the propensity to innovate in China's large- and medium-sized industrial enterprises. *China: An International Journal*, 5(2), 228–249.

Cheung, K-Y and P Lin (2004). Spillover effects of FDI on innovation in China: Evidence from the provincial data. *China Economic Review*, 15(1), 25–44.

Chuang, Y-C and P-F Hsu (2004). FDI, trade, and spillover efficiency: Evidence from China's manufacturing sector. *Applied Economics*, 36, 1103–1115.

Conyon, S, S Girma, S Thompson and P Wrights (2002). The impact of foreign acquisition on wages and productivity in the U.K. *Journal of Industrial Economics*, 50, 85–102.

Djankov, S and B Hoekman (2000). Foreign investment and productivity growth in Czech enterprises. *World Bank Economic Review*, 14, 49–64.

Dollar, D, M Hallward-Driemeier and TA Mengistae (2006). Investment climate and international integration. *World Development*, 34(9), 1498–1516.

Feenstra, RC and GH Hanson (1997). Foreign direct investment and relative wages: Evidence from Mexico's maquiladoras. *Journal of International Economics*, 42(3–4), 371–393.

Fosfuri, A, M Motta and T Rønde (2001). Foreign direct investment and spillovers through workers' mobility. *Journal of International Economics*, 53(1), 205–222.

Fung, KC, H Iizaka and SY Tong (2004). FDI in China: Policy, recent trend and impact. *Global Economic Review*, 32(2), 99–130.

Ge, Y and Y Chen (2008). Foreign ownership and productivity of joint ventures. *Economic Development and Cultural Change*, 56, 895–920.

Girma, S and H Görg (2007). Evaluating the foreign ownership wage premium using a difference-in-differences matching approach. *Journal of International Economics*, 72(1), 97–112.

Glass, A and K Saggi (2002). Multinational firms and technology transfer. *Scandinavian Journal of Economics*, 104(4), 495–513.

Görg, H and D Greenaway (2004). Much ado about nothing? Do domestic firms really benefit from foreign direct investment? *World Bank Research Observer*, 19(2), 171–197.

Greene, WH (ed.) (2008). *Econometric Analysis*, 6th edn., Upper Saddle River, N.J.: Prentice Hall.

Grossman, G and E Helpman (1991a). Quality ladders and product cycles. *Quarterly Journal of Economics*, 106(2): 557–586.

Grossman, G and E Helpman (1991b). Quality ladders in the theory of growth. *Review of Economic Studies*, 58(1), 43–61.

Gupta, N (2005). Partial privatization and firm performance. *Journal of Finance*, 60(2), 987–1015.

Haaker, M (1999). Spillovers from foreign direct investment through labour turnover: The supply of management skills. Discussion Paper, London School of Economics.

Haddad, M and AE Harrison (1993). Are there positive spillovers from direct foreign investment? Evidence from panel data for Morocco. *Journal of Development Economics*, 42(1), 51–74.

Hale, G and C Long. Did foreign direct investment put an upward pressure on wages in China? IMF Economic Review, Forthcoming.

Hale, G and C Long (2011). Are there productivity spillovers from foreign direct investment in China? *Pacific Economic Review*, 16(2), 135–153.

Hallak, JC and J Sivadasan (2006). Productivity, quality and exporting behavior under minimum quality requirements. Mimeo, Presented at LACEA 2007.

Hallward-Driemeier, M, SJ Wallsten and LC Xu (2003). The investment climate and the firm: Firm-level evidence from China. World Bank Policy Research Working Paper No. 3003.

Hasan, R (2002). The impact of imported and domestic technologies on the productivity of firms: Panel data evidence from Indian manufacturing firms. *Journal of Development Economics*, 69(1/2), 23–49.

Haskel, JE, SC Pereira and MJ Slaughter (2007). Does inward foreign direct investment boost the productivity of domestic firms? *The Review of Economics and Statistics*, 89(3) 482–496.

Helpman, E, MJ Melitz and SR Yeaple (2004). Export versus FDI with heterogeneous firms. *American Economic Review*, 94(1), 300–316.

Heyman, F, F Sjöholm and PG Tingvall (2007). Is there really a foreign ownership wage premium? Evidence from matched employer–employee data. *Journal of International Economics*, 73(2), 355–376.

Hu, AG and GH Jefferson (2002). FDI impact and spillover: Evidence from China's electronic and textile industries. *The World Economy*, 25(8), 1063–1076.

Huang, J-T (2004). Spillovers from Taiwan, Hong Kong, and Macau investment and from other foreign investment in Chinese industries. *Contemporary Economic Policy*, 22(1), 13–25.

Huang, Y (2005). *Selling China: Foreign Direct Investment During the Reform Era*, Cambridge Modern China Series. Cambridge, New York, and Melbourne: Cambridge University Press.

Huggins, R, M Demirbag and VI Ratcheva (2007). Global knowledge and R&D foreign direct investment flows: Recent patterns in Asia Pacific, Europe, and North America. *International Review of Applied Economics*, 21(3), 437–451.

Javorcik, BS (2004). Does foreign direct investment increase the productivity of domestic firms? In search of spillovers through backward linkages. *American Economic Review*, 94(3), 605–627.

Javorcik, BS (2008). Can survey evidence shed light on spillovers from foreign direct investment? *World Bank Research Observer*, 23(2), 139–159.

Karpaty, P (2007). Productivity effects of foreign acquisitions in Swedish manufacturing: The FDI productivity issue revisited. *International Journal of the Economics of Business*, 14(2), 241–260.

Kato, T and C Long (2006). Executive compensation, firm performance, and corporate governance in China: Evidence from firms listed in the Shanghai and Shenzhen Stock Exchanges. *Economic Development and Cultural Change*, 54(4), 945–983.

Kaufmann, L (1997). A model of spillovers through labor recruitment. *International Economic Journal*, 11(3), 13–33.

Keller, W and S Yeaple (2009). Multinational enterprises, international trade, and productivity growth: Firm-level evidence from the United States. The Review of Economics and Statistics, 91(4), 821–831.

Kneller, R and M Pisu (2007). Industrial linkages and export spillovers from FDI. *The World Economy*, 30(1), 105–134.

Kokko, A, M Zejan and R Tanzini (2001). Trade regimes and spillover effects of FDI: Evidence from Uruguay. *Weltwirschaftliches Archiv*, 137(1), 124–149.

Lane, J, RE Feinberg and H Broadman (2002). Do labour strategies matter? An analysis of two enterprise-level data sets in China. *International Journal of the Economics of Business*, 9(2), 225–237.

Levinsohn, J and A Petrin (2003). Estimating production functions using inputs to control for unobservables. *Review of Economic Studies*, 70(243), 317–341.

Li, J, C Zhou and EJ Zajac (2009). Control, collaboration, and productivity in international joint ventures: Theory and evidence. *Strategic Management Journal*, 30(8), 865–884.

Li, X, X Liu and D Parker (2001). Foreign direct investment and productivity spillovers in the Chinese manufacturing sector. *Economic Systems*, 25(4), 305–321.

Lipsey, R and F Sjöholm (2004). Foreign direct investment, education and wages in Indonesian manufacturing. *Journal of Development Economics*, 73(1), 415–422.

Liu, X, D Parker, K Vaidya and Y Wei (2001). The impact of foreign direct investment on labour productivity in the Chinese electronics industry. *International Business Review*, 10(4), 421–439.

Liu, Z (2002). Foreign direct investment and technology spillover: Evidence from China. *Journal of Comparative Economics*, 30(3), 579–602.

Liu, Z (2008). Foreign direct investment and technology spillovers: Theory and evidence. *Journal of Development Economics*, 85(1/2), 176–193.

Ma, A (2006). Export spillovers to Chinese firms: Evidence from provincial data. *Journal of Chinese Economic and Business Studies*, 4(2), 127–149.

Mayneris, F and S Poncet (2010). Export performance of China's domestic firms: The role of foreign export spillovers. CEPII Working Paper 2010-32.

Melitz, MJ (2003). The impact of trade on intra-industry reallocations and aggregate industry productivity. *Econometrica*, 71(6), 1695–1725.

Moran, TH (2006). *Harnessing Foreign Direct Investment for Development: Policies for Developed and Developing Countries.* Washington D.C.: Center for Global Development.

Moulton, BR (1990). An illustration of a pitfall in estimating the effects of aggregate variables on micro-units. *The Review of Economics and Statistics*, 72(2), 334–338.

Naughton, B (2007). *Transitions and Growth.* Cambridge, M.A.: MIT Press.

Ng, LF-Y and C Tuan (2005). Industry technology performance of manufacturing FDI: Micro-level evidence from joint ventures in China. *International Journal of Technology Management*, 32(3/4), 246–263.

Olley, GS and A Pakes (1996). The dynamics of productivity in the telecommunications equipment industry. *Econometrica*, 64(6), 1263–1297.

Peri, G and D Urban (2006). Catching-up to foreign technology? Evidence on the "Veblen-Gerschenkron" effect of foreign investment. Regional Science and Urban Economics, 36(1), 72–98.

Rodriguez-Clare, A (1996). Multinationals, linkages, and economic development. *American Economic Review*, 86(4), 852–873.

Ruane, F and J Sutherland (2005). Foreign direct investment and export spillovers: How do export platforms fare? IIIS Discussion Paper 58.

Sargan, JD (1958). The estimation of economic relationships using instrumental variables. *Econometrica*, 26(3), 393–415.

Sargan, JD (1959). The estimation of relationships with autocorrelated residuals by the use of instrumental variables. *Journal of the Royal Statistical Society B*, 21, 91–105.

Schoors, K and B van der Tol (2002). The productivity effect of foreign ownership on domestic firms in Hungary. University of Gent Working Paper 157.

Sun, Q, W Tong and Q Yu (2002). Determinants of foreign direct investment across China. *Journal of International Money and Finance*, 21, 79–113.

Swenson, DL (2008). Multinationals and the creation of Chinese trade linkages. *Canadian Journal of Economics*, 41(2), 596–618.

Takii, S (2004). Productivity differentials between local and foreign plants in Indonesian manufacturing, 1995. *World Development*, 32(11), 1957–1969.

Taylor, MS (1994). TRIPs, trade, and growth. *International Economic Review*, 35(2), 361–381.

Wang, J-Y and M Blomström (1992). Foreign investment and technology transfer: A simple model. *European Economic Review*, 36(1), 137–155.

Wei, Y and X Liu (2006). Productivity spillovers from R&D, exports and FDI in China's manufacturing sector. *Journal of International Business Studies*, 37(4), 544–557.

Yasar, M and CJM Paul (2007). International linkages and productivity at the plant level: Foreign direct investment, exports, imports and licensing. *Journal of International Economics*, 71(2), 373–388.

Index